CYNTHIA RENÉ DOSS

That Quiet Voice

A MEMOIR OF HOPE

Published by Muses and Graces Publishing, Los Angeles

Print ISBN: 978-1-54392-959-1

www.cynthiadoss.com

To Renatè, with love

ACKNOWLEDGMENTS

I am fortunate to have discovered the Creative Writing Certificate Program at the University of California, Los Angeles. The instructors are accomplished writers who generously share their talents in a supportive atmosphere. Specifically, thank you to Daniel Jaffe, Shawna Kenney, Jenny Nash, Rochelle Shapiro, Liz Gonzàlez, Ellis Weiner, Harry Youtt, Judy Prager, Deb Borofka, Victoria Zacheim, Sharon Bray and Mieke Eerkens. You helped me elevate my writing skill to a higher level.

To my friends, Valerie Black and Paula Schaefer, who suffered through some pretty rough first drafts, I appreciate your patience and encouragement. I am also grateful to my healthcare professionals, including Dr. Michelle Ryan, Dr. Steven Mee, Dr. Nancy Godfrey, Dr. Susan Sklar, Dr. Stephen Brown, Dr. Tara Scott, Dr. George Macer, and Dr. Sally Kim. Like Humpty-Dumpty, you helped put me back together again.

Finally, to my sister Renatè. You will always be my hero.

PROLOGUE

I am standing in the open doorway of an airplane 12,000 feet in the air, ready to jump. I didn't tell any friends or family my plans in advance. I suspected they would try to talk me out of it. But now I'm thinking: *Why are you here? What the hell possessed you to try something so drastic?*

I am not a risk taker. I've worked for the same employer for over thirty years, I use double bags to take out the garbage, I never exceed the speed limit on the freeway, and most importantly—I am deathly afraid of heights. Yet, here I stand, ready to jump.

Cool air brushes softly across my cheeks. The roar of the plane's engine pounds against my eardrums and the vibration of the plane jerks my body from side to side. I plant my feet at the edge of the doorway to try to steady myself. Greg, my instructor is tethered to my back. My knees are locked beneath me. I hear Greg say, "All you need to do is take one step. I'll do the rest." A cold sweat washes over me. There is a knot in the pit of my stomach. And my mind is racing without perceptible thoughts.

"Don't be nervous, you can do this," Greg says.

Suddenly, my mind is clear with the exception of one thought: *You've wanted to do this for months. It's showtime!*

A surprising calm comes over me. I shake my head, adjust my shoulders and step away from the plane. My quest for answers had begun. In the end, I would learn what compelled me to take such a dramatic step; to risk everything. It began one fateful night seven years earlier.

THE CALL

A loud noise rang in my head. I opened my eyes to a dark room. I assumed the noise was my alarm clock, so I smacked the top of it, knocking it off the nightstand. When the noise didn't stop, I looked at my backup alarm clock. It was only 3 am, too soon for the alarm to be ringing. Then I realized it was the telephone. I answered in a gruff voice,

"Hello?"

"Hey, it's me." It was my sister, Renatè. Her voice was barely audible.

"Hey, what's up?" I asked, trying to keep a light tone though I knew if she were calling at that hour it was for a serious reason.

"I have sickle cell pain and I'm on my way to the emergency room. I'll call you tomorrow."

Renatè had been battling Sickle Cell Anemia (SCA) since she was an infant. In a SCA crisis, normal disk-shaped red blood cells change to the shape of a sickle. The sickle shaped cells carry less oxygen and tend to clog veins, further depriving the body of life sustaining oxygen. The result for the patient is excruciating pain. It is estimated that over 80,000 African Americans suffer from SCA. In the 1960's when Renatè was diagnosed, most SCA patients didn't live beyond their 20's. At age 38, Renatè had beaten the odds.

I hung up the phone and the dead silence of night confronted me. *"How could she be sick?"* I thought. We were in the Bahamas on vacation the previous week and she had been fine. She seemed a little tired, but that was what the vacation was for—relaxation. I lay flat on my back, staring up at the florescent stars mounted on my bedroom ceiling. I stared for an hour and tried to occupy my mind with figuring out the constellations. As hard as I tried, I couldn't escape the dread that was slowly grabbing hold of me.

Some SCA patients have to be hospitalized to get their pain under control. Renatè hated hospitals. She chose to deal with her condition on her own. She had pain medication and used hot compresses on whatever part of her body the disease attacked. I knew she had to be in bad condition to volunteer to go to a hospital, and that thought haunted me to the point where I finally gave up on the constellations. Instead, I rolled over, covered my face with my pillow, and cried.

12 HOURS IN HELL

The next day was torturous. I started calling Renatè as soon as I got to work. I left several messages throughout the morning but got no response. I was an event manager with a wedding reception to oversee that day. I busied myself making sure that the arrangements were perfect, but my pleasant smile masked the growing anxiety I felt inside. While I waited, I tried to go about my duties as if I weren't faced with impending doom. When afternoon came and I hadn't heard from Renatè, I decided to take action. Being born two years before her gave me license to go into big sister mode. I was 1,400 miles away, which put me at a disadvantage. It was time to call in the cavalry, so I called the police department where she lived in Wichita, Kansas.

"WPD, this is Officer Barnaby speaking, how may I help you?"

Words flew out of my mouth as if they had been shot from a cannon. "My name is Cynthia Doss. I'm calling about my sister Renatè. She called me last night. She said that she was on her way to the emergency room and she'd call me today. It's been twelve hours and I haven't heard from her. I've called her apartment, but get no answer...I don't know if she's sick and can't answer the phone or if they kept her in the hospital. And directory assistance wouldn't give me the names of hospitals in Wichita. I'm in California, so I can't check on her myself. I don't know what else to do."

There was a moment of silence.

"Okay, ma'am, just calm down. You say your sister told you she was going to the hospital?"

"Yes, she was supposed to call me today but I haven't heard from her."

"Give me her address. I'll send a patrol car to her apartment. And if you have a pen handy, I can give you the names of our hospitals. I'll call you as soon we know more."

I scribbled the names of the hospitals and thanked him for his help. When I got off the phone, one of the event staff called me over the two-way radio. The bride and groom had arrived. I ran downstairs so that I could assist with their grand entrance into the reception, but my heart was racing so fast that I needed to pause for a moment and compose myself before entering the lobby. We lined up the wedding party; they proceeded inside as the room erupted in applause.

It was such a joyous day for the wedding couple. The florist had expertly decorated the venue with stunning arrangements. The wedding cake was a tiered marvel trimmed in flowers. Cute little favors designed and made by the bride surrounded the floral arrangements on each guest table. Though I was happy for the couple and their prospect for a bright future, my immediate future was uncertain and shrouded in despair. As soon as the doors shut behind the wedding party, I ran back upstairs to my office to see if they found my sister. I was only there a few minutes when I heard the phone ring.

"Ms. Doss, this is Officer Barnaby. Our officers checked your sister's apartment. She wasn't home but they left a message for your sister to call you as soon as possible. I wish I could do more."

"You've helped me tremendously", I said. "Thank you so much."

As soon as I finished talking to Officer Barnaby, I started calling the hospitals. None of the three of them had a record of Renatè as an admission. I was frantic. I thought of my parents. Ordinarily, I would turn to them for advice, but calling them before I knew what happened to Renatè would only upset them. I also wasn't sure exactly where they were; only that they were on a United Methodist retreat somewhere. What could I do? At that moment of indecision, my phone rang again.

This time it was Renatè's friend, Patricia.

"I stopped by Renatè's apartment to let Sweet Pea out and saw the note from the police," she said. Sweet Pea was my sister's Chihuahua. "Renatè was admitted to St. Vincent Hospital," she said. "Didn't Angela call you?" Angela was another friend of Renatè's.

"No, I haven't heard anything since Renatè called last night."

"Angela was supposed to call and tell you that Renatè was admitted to St. Vincent Hospital. I guess she must have gone home and went to bed instead."

I was furious. Not only had Angela abandoned Renatè at the hospital, but she didn't even call to update me. How irresponsible! But I didn't want to waste my energy being angry. I had to focus on the present. I told Patricia I'd be on the first flight out of Los Angeles Airport in the morning and she agreed to pick me up at the airport in Wichita.

I rushed home and while scurrying from room to room, pulling clothes out of the closet and drawers, I dialed my oldest brother, Cyril's phone number.

"Renatè is at St. Vincent Hospital," I said when he answered.

"Is it Sickle Cell?"

"Yeah. I need to find Mommy and Daddy. They're at a United Methodist retreat somewhere, but I don't know what city they're in." This was the perfect task for Cyril, an amateur sleuth, and one less thing for me to worry about.

"I'll get on the Internet and see if I can locate them," he said.

By the time I tucked the last pair of socks away in my suitcase, Cyril called back.

"I found them at Baker University. They are going to drive home to Junction City, and then they'll head for Wichita. They should be there tomorrow afternoon. I have a few things to clear up at work, but I'll get on the road as soon as I can."

It would be a long drive from Minnesota, but I was relieved that Cyril was coming. His relationship with Renatè was tenuous. My mother's greatest wish was that we would remain close as adults. After all, her siblings were her best friends and she wanted that type of relationship for us. But something happened in the past that drove a wedge between Cyril and Renatè. Neither one of them would say why they didn't get along. I loved them and had a good relationship with both of them. If I were to speculate on the problem, I'd say it was because one was the oldest and the other, the youngest. Or more likely, it could have been because they were each fiercely independent and headstrong. However, in a crisis their differences weren't important and any animosity no longer mattered. That's what I love about my family.

DAY 1

When I arrived at the hospital, I proceeded to the sixth floor nurse's station like Patricia had instructed me. But when I asked for Renatè, they told me she had been moved to the intensive care unit, or ICU. Upon hearing that news, my knees weakened beneath me and it felt like someone had punched me in the stomach. ICU? In all the years of dealing with her condition, she had never been that sick before.

On the elevator ride up to ICU, I tried to compose myself. I was afraid of what condition I might find her in, but I knew I couldn't show that I was upset. After all, I was her big sister. I was the one that always assured her that everything would be all right. She needed me to be strong. I took a deep breath, squared my shoulders, and stepped off the elevator.

Bright lights illuminated the room's white walls and cabinets so powerfully they hurt my eyes. An assortment of supply jars of varying heights lined the countertops. I placed my overnight bag on the turquoise vinyl chair in the corner. Above the chair, a dry erase board reported:

July 13, 1997

Day – Margie, Night – Becky

Weight: 95.3

Renatè lay motionless, cocooned in a bed sheet with her arms straight at her side. The bed was positioned in the middle of the room. An oxygen mask covered her nose and mouth. Tubes and wires connected her arms to three machines. The whir of the machines calibrating, dispensing fluids, and monitoring her vital signs filled the air. The syncopated rhythm changed my heartbeat to match its ominous sound. My chest tightened to the point that my arms barely moved. It hurt to breathe.

Renatè approached life as if she were leading a conga line. A clinical psychologist by profession, she normally exemplified the youthful spirit of the children and adolescents she treated. Now, her dance card was blank. I took a deep breath and walked to the bed.

Her eyes darted around the room, not focusing on anything in particular. The squeak of my tennis shoes on the polished linoleum floor caught her attention.

"Cynthia!" The mask muffled her voice.

"Hey, there, how ya doin'?" It sounded so stupid to ask under the circumstances.

"It hurts," she said. "It hurts really bad."

I took both her hands in mine. It was like touching an oven, they were so hot.

"Where does it hurt?"

"My legs." She moved her knees as though she were walking. "It's bad," she repeated before removing the oxygen mask. "When

I…there wasn't anyone left…Houston…can you bring me a bowling ball, please?"

I nodded, but I didn't understand her. Her eyes continued to move and occasionally roll back in her head. I took another deep breath to prevent myself from crying. A morphine drip was connected to her I.V. I pushed the pump to administer a dose. Her eyes blinked slowly.

"You can rest now. I'm here," I told her as I put the oxygen mask back on her face.

I watched her as she slept. A harsh gurgling sound came from her throat like a partially clogged drain. The vibration of her breathing and the rhythm of the machines made me shudder.

I stroked her forearm and wiped her brow. She inherited my mother's baby soft skin. Her complexion was chestnut brown and clear of blemishes. She had a small mole on the side of her lower lip that gave her a Liz Taylor kind of quality. Without make-up, she was beautiful, but when she applied shadow, her naturally expressive eyes opened up like a peacock spreading its plume.

I looked down at the way I was dressed. In my haste to leave town, I just threw some clothes together. I was wearing a Foghorn Leghorn t-shirt and jeans with threadbare knees. One of Renate's greatest joys was making fun of the way I dressed. I once had a tie dyed pink, orange and electric blue T-shirt and matching pants and when I wore the outfit, she apologized to her friends saying, "Please excuse the way my sister dresses, she lives in California."

Ordinarily, she would delight in teasing me, but that night, she was silent instead. Because she couldn't see me, now I could cry. I reached for a box of tissues on the counter, and noticed there was writing on the bottom of the box. In big bold numbers in my sister's handwriting was my home phone number—I cried harder.

When my parents arrived several hours later, I quickly dried my tears. I didn't want to upset them. I motioned for them to stay in the hallway and then joined them. Daddy wore a short-sleeved dress shirt and khaki trousers. I felt the pens in his pocket protector as I hugged him. We often teased him about being a geek for using a pocket protector, but he proudly defended this practice as a sign of intelligence. I could also feel the stubble of his five-o'clock shadow as our cheeks brushed past each other. Mommy wore a simple tunic and slacks. The sweet smell of her signature perfume—Estee Lauder Private Collection—was comforting. Mommy was the best at hugging. She could hug you so tight your joints popped and you didn't care, because it meant everything was going to be alright.

"You may not be able to understand her," I cautioned. "I don't know if it's the pain or the meds they have her on, but she's not making any sense." I clasped my hands in front of me to keep them from shaking. I twirled the ring on my left hand the way I always do when I'm nervous. "I've never seen her like this before."

My parents nodded and we approached her bedside. Daddy gently shook her foot, the same way he used to wake us up in the morning. Renatè's eyes opened for a few minutes.

"Everything's gonna be okay, buddy," he said.

"Can you folks step outside, please?" the nurse interrupted. "We need to connect her to a ventilator."

As we stood in the hallway, Mommy was uncharacteristically quiet. She held her purse on her left arm, both elbows squeezed close to her sides as if she were trying to hold herself together. I looked at my watch repeatedly, but nothing happened.

Finally, Dr. Hartley emerged from Renatè's room. She was a slender woman in her forties with long brown hair, red framed eyeglasses, and an earnest look on her oval face. Her lips parted slightly as she attempted to smile and introduced herself.

"Mr. and Mrs. Doss, I want to be candid with you. Your daughter's condition is serious. She has pneumonia, her liver enzymes are too low, she has blood in her lungs and abdomen, her kidneys are not functioning properly, and she has an infection that's not responding to antibiotics. Also her hematocrit, which determines the percentage of red blood cells in her system, is 8. Normal hematocrit is 13 – 14."

We stood there unable to talk, barely able to digest this enormous amount of information. I finally asked, "What can you do for her?"

"I've ordered a blood transfusion in hopes that it will dilute the percentage of sickle cells in her blood. We're putting her on dialysis and the ventilator will help her breathe. We'll continue to try different antibiotics, but I have to be honest with you. If we can't fight the infection, her organs will not be able to recover. Has she had any recent illnesses or injury?"

"No. We were just on vacation last week and she was fine."

"What about previous hospitalizations?"

"She was in the hospital about five years ago in Houston."

"What were her symptoms?"

"She had pneumonia, but she didn't go into SCA crisis. Renatè's friend, Barbara, works in medical records where she was hospitalized. I could see if she can fax Renatè's records to you."

"That would be very helpful," Dr. Hartley said. "Do you have any other questions?"

We looked at each other and shook our heads, still trying to process the information.

"Have a seat in the waiting room and I'll have the nurses let you know when they are finished," Dr. Hartley told us.

We retreated to the waiting room, which looked like an abandoned classroom. A dozen worn brown burlap-covered chairs stood in disarray. Crumpled tissues and paper cups littered the floor. The tables were cluttered with toys and unfinished puzzles. My mother sat wringing her hands and staring at the floor. I wanted to cry, but it wouldn't have been appropriate. Our family doesn't cry in public because it upsets other people. As soon as my mother regained her composure, she pelted me with a barrage of questions.

"What did you and Renatè do in the Bahamas?"

"We walked on the beach and shopped in the stores mostly."

"What did you eat? What did you drink? Were you partying?"

"No, we weren't partying. And most of our meals were just American food. We only tried one of the local delicacies—conch— but neither of us liked it."

"Did you stay out late at night?"

"No. We were back in the hotel room fairly early and we slept late in the mornings."

"Why didn't you do a better job of taking care of Renatè?"

"We didn't do anything out of the ordinary last week. I ate the same things Renatè did and I feel fine."

"But you know her system is delicate. She can't tolerate the same things you can."

I wasn't going to argue with my mother, but I found it hard to believe that we had done anything in the Bahamas that would expose Renatè to danger. Though I thought it was unfair of her to blame me for Renatè's condition, there was a kernel of doubt about my declaration deep inside me, but I couldn't allow it to grow.

Both restless and wanting to get away from the game of *20 Questions* with my mother, I excused myself to find a pay phone to call Barbara. After explaining Renatè's current situation to her, Barbara agreed to fax St. Vincent a copy of her medical records.

Walking back to Renatè's room, the memory of our trip to the Bahamas the week before was fresh on my mind.

BAHAMA MAMAS

Renatè and I had usually only seen each other for brief periods at our parents' home during the holidays, but now we were going to cruise to the Bahamas together and spend the weekend. I was giddy at the prospect of spending three days and two nights alone with my sister, my best friend.

It had been late in the afternoon when I arrived at the hotel in St. Petersburg, Florida, and Renatè was due to arrive in a couple of hours, which meant there was just enough time to arrange a surprise. She'd had her 38th birthday a few weeks before and with us living in different states, it had been years since I was able to celebrate with her. This year would be special.

I hailed a cab and asked the driver where I could find a birthday cake. He said I could try a nearby deli, which turned out to be a good choice. The deli had a fresh batch of cupcakes and fortunately for me, birthday candles as well.

When Renatè arrived, her normally coiffed hair was windblown and she had a flustered expression on her face. "Man what a trip," she greeted. "I thought I'd never get here." She tossed her luggage on the bed and gave me a big hug. Then she went into the bathroom to freshen up. I lit the candle and hid the cupcake behind my back. When she came out of the bathroom, I stretched out my arms.

"Ta da! Happy birthday to you. Happy birthday to you. Happy birthday, dear Renatè. Happy birthday to you."

"That's nice," she said in a quiet voice. I waited for an awkward moment before she leaned over and blew out the candle. This was not the response I expected—and certainly not worth a $14 cab ride. She must have sensed my disappointment and said, "I'm sorry, I'm just tired. I'll be better after I get some rest."

Renatè's declaration meant little at the time. After all, we were both tired. Work had ground us to a pulp and the purpose of this trip was to rest and rejuvenate. How could I have known the extent of her fatigue?

When I returned to Renatè's room, the nurses had finished connecting her to the ventilator. I pulled the chair to the side of the bed and sat holding her hand. Her eyes were closed, her face relaxed. The sheets were neatly tucked around her body.

She looked so small and vulnerable. It was as if she was ten years old again, and I was reminded of how I used to sit by her side back then. She would lay there holding on tightly to Dragony, a stuffed purple dragon that was her constant companion, its neck wobbly from being hugged so much. I would refill her hot water bottle when necessary and rub her arm or her leg, whichever part of her body was in pain from the SCA. I'd made sure she always had something to drink, because it was important for her to stay hydrated. Also, I did silly things to make her laugh, anything to distract her from the pain.

At a young age, the genetics behind SCA were explained to me. Both my parents carry the trait and with four children, our family matched the statistical probability for the disease. Two of us, my brothers Cyril and Curtis inherited the trait—which they could pass on to their children—while one of us, Renatè, has the disease, and one has nothing—me. And because I have nothing, I decided early on that it would always be my responsibility to take care of Renatè.

DAY 2

July 14, 1997

Day – Margie, Night – Becky

Weight: 93.3

On the second day, Patricia came to visit. She knew I had only brought an overnight bag and offered to take me shopping. Fortunately for me, Kohls Department Store was having a clearance sale. I selected several tops and when I found a pair of purple jeans, I held them up and smiled. Since purple was Renatè's favorite color, this would certainly meet with her approval.

After our shopping trip, I stayed by Renatè's side around the clock. The only way I knew it was morning or evening was from the arrival and departure of my parents. They spent the night at Renatè's apartment, and though Daddy would come into the room periodically to check on her, Mommy was conspicuously absent. From the time Renatè fell silent, Mommy never entered her hospital room.

Because Renatè was unconscious, I felt she needed an advocate. It wasn't that I didn't have faith in the medical staff—they were competent and professional. But I had an experience that taught me Renatè needed someone to speak up for her.

The night before, a medical technician came into her room. She must not have seen me sitting in the chair in the corner, because she was startled when I said hello.

"I'm going to draw some blood," the technician said, and I approached the bed to watch. I watched as she inserted the needle into Renatè's arm several times, but couldn't get a vein. "I'll try a butterfly needle," she told me, but even with the butterfly needle, she was unsuccessful.

"Is it possible to get someone else to try?" I asked.

Her face turned red and her eyes darted around rather than making contact with mine. "I guess I could call my supervisor," she finally mumbled.

"Please do." I often think about what would have happened if I hadn't been there to make this request. Would she have just continued to jab needles in Renatè's arm because she couldn't respond? Fortunately, her supervisor ended up sending another technician, who was able to successfully draw Renatè's blood without a problem.

Renatè laid motionless, eyes closed with no expression on her face. I lifted her arm to hold her hand, but there was no resistance. The only motion in her body was her chest, which rose and fell with each breath of the ventilator. I wrapped her fingers around mine. I thought about how much she was like my mother. She had inherited Mommy's long and slender fingers and her nails were expertly painted purple. Seeing her hands reminded me of an incident from many years ago.

We were still children, and our oldest brother was around twelve. Mommy took my two brothers, sister, and I shopping in our Rambler station wagon. When Mommy started to close the garage door, a car drove by and distracted, she looked in that direction. As a result, instead of grabbing the garage door handle, her right hand went between the wooden slats. The door came down, smashing her fingers. Realizing her mistake, she somehow managed to lift the door and pulled her hand out, blood was gushing from the wound.

"Cyril," she said calmly to my brother. "Go inside and call your Daddy. Tell him that I hurt my hand and I'm on the way to Irwin Army Hospital." She then turned to my other brother. "Curtis, go inside and get me a towel."

My brothers rushed inside, did as they were asked, and then returned to the car. Mommy wrapped her hand with the towel, but the blood seeped through the fabric quickly, creating a mess. She then slid behind the wheel and drove to the hospital, guiding the steering wheel with her good hand. No one spoke a word in the car; our usual arguments about who touched whom or who hit whom were silenced. We were too stunned. I couldn't take my eyes off of the white towel as it continued to turn completely crimson. Mommy must have been in pain, but she didn't display any emotion. Looking back, it's possible that she was in shock.

We arrived at the emergency room and they immediately took Mommy into an examination room. The skin on her fingers was mangled and required numerous stitches, but miraculously, no bones were broken. The beds of her nails remained black for a while, but eventually, her fingers healed without a single scar.

I thought about it later and wondered why my mother didn't call an ambulance instead of making the thirty-minute drive to the hospital. I concluded that it was a testament to her fortitude and self-reliance. After so many years as an Army wife—and almost a single parent at times—she had learned how to fend for herself. Driving herself to the hospital was a natural response, but to me, as a child witnessing what seemed like a terrible injury, what she did was extraordinary. By remaining calm, she kept us from being upset. Had it not been for her thoughtfulness, the event could have left us traumatized.

Now I would have to follow my mother's example. The uncertainty of Renatè's situation was scary. SCA had never made her this sick before, and I wondered about what could have caused such a severe reaction. When we were children, we had to be careful not to play too rough with Renatè because any bruise on her flesh could cause a crisis. This time, instead of a bruise, her internal organs were fighting the disease. But how could this have happened? My mother's questions came back to me. *Did* we do something in the Bahamas that caused her illness? Was I responsible for not taking better care of her? When she was a child, I could protect her from injury, but as a grown woman, she was capable of making her own choices. I couldn't control her environment.

Despite my claims to my mother of the contrary, there was a feeling deep inside me that I might have been able to prevent her illness. I knew she was tired during our time in the Bahamas. Should I have insisted she rest more? The thought that I might have been responsible for her current state made me shudder. I wanted to cry, but refused. If I were going to handle this situation with poise, I would have to be strong. Blubbering at that point would have served no positive purpose.

A quiet voice inside told me, *"You can do this. You can face anything"*. I remembered the self-reliance my mother exhibited in a scary situation and imagined that I could muster the courage necessary to deal with whatever was to come.

Each day, I recorded the news from her doctors in a journal. At the time, I wanted to chronicle her progress, though in hindsight it was really to help me keep my sanity. A parade of doctors was treating her—a hematologist, gastroenterologist, nephrologists, pulmonologist, infectious disease specialist, and a senior physician responsible for overseeing all of her care. They came and went at all hours of the day and night, so the journal helped me keep track of each of their assessments of her condition.

That night, I retreated to the waiting room, the recliner in the corner a welcome refuge. In what eventually would became a nightly ritual, I turned on the television to TV Land, where I could escape into the wacky world of Oliver and Lisa on *Green Acres* or a dusty cattle drive on *Bonanza*. Watching shows from my childhood like *Petticoat Junction*, *The Beverly Hillbillies*, *My Favorite Martian*, and *The Andy Griffith Show* allowed me to laugh for a few moments. And *Gunsmoke* was especially reassuring, because the good guys always won.

PRETTY IN PURPLE

The color purple has always been Renatè's fascination. I have never met anyone who identifies more strongly with a color. Everything she owns is purple, and after years of buying her presents in that color, I began to like it and started surrounding myself with it. I still like fuchsia, but the color purple reminds me to always keep Renatè in my prayers.

Renatè's affinity for purple is just part of what makes her unique. Another unique thing she does is using her own expressions. For some reason, she can't pronounce cubic zirconia, and so ends up calling them "chromium zucchinis." She calls sexually transmitted diseases "epizooty of the booty." And one of her favorite expressions is, "If you like it, I love it."

Renatè never let SCA rule her life. She earned a Bachelor's degree in Psychology and a Master's degree in Education. At the time of her hospitalization, she was working full-time as Director of Programs for Wichita Children's Home. I could tell from the time I spent in her work environment that she was loved by the children and respected by her co-workers. She once described one of the more recalcitrant youth as having the attention span of a gnat on crack, but she loved her work and cared deeply about all of the children in her care. She is a realist that prefers to see the glass as half-full instead of half-empty.

Renatè occupies a special part of my heart. We grew up with the same values. We developed separate personalities despite having interests that were similar. Her nickname in college was Sunshine, and if she was the sun, I was the stars; we each shone in our own way. We both enjoyed a wide variety of music, but still argued over who was better—Michael Jackson or Prince. I favored Prince. She said she didn't trust a man that wore more makeup than she did.

Like our grandmother before us, we both were fans of what used to be All Star Wrestling and is now World Wrestling Entertainment. There is something about physically buff men in tights bouncing around the ring that is oddly entertaining, a unique blend of athleticism and showmanship. Each week, new rivalries were played out. John Cena, The Rock, Batista, Shawn Michaels and Triple H, versus Andre the Giant, The Undertaker, Randy Orton, Edge and Kane. The perpetual battle between the good guys and the bad guys raged on. It was a refreshing release to yell at the television when the bad guy hid his dirty tricks from the clueless referee. I knew not to ever call Renatè during a wrestling match because she wouldn't answer the phone. She didn't let anything interfere with her enjoyment of a match. I once hinted that the matches might be staged—meaning the winner was predetermined —and Renatè responded as if I had said Jesus was never resurrected from the dead.

We also shared a love of action movies and British murder mysteries. No chick flicks for us; we like adrenaline-fueled car chases, martial arts matches, and explosions—*lots* of explosions. A favorite series is *The Transporter* movies (the first and third in the series primarily; the second was a stunning disappointment), and we enjoy the exploits of Sherlock Holmes and Hercule Poirot. Renatè has the mind of a sleuth and can always guess the murderer while I am usually clueless.

So if Renatè were gone, who would tease me about my choice in music and in clothes? Who else would gossip with me for hours? Her presence brought joy into my life, and if she were to leave, I was afraid I would never experience joy ever again.

DAY 3

July 15, 1997

Day – Margie, Night –Becky

Weight: 91.1

The next morning, I awoke to an empty waiting room. The recliner that allowed me to rest my weary bones had been surprisingly comfortable, and I was able to sleep soundly in it. I looked at the clock and saw that it was almost 7 am. I didn't want to miss the doctors making their rounds, so I bolted to my sister's room. I paused in the doorway to allow my eyes to adjust from the dark of the waiting room to the stark lighting of the hallway. As I passed other patients in the ICU, I couldn't help but notice that they were all elderly. Many of them could have been facing the final days of their lives. Renatè hadn't reached forty yet; her life was just beginning. It didn't seem fair.

When I walked into Renatè's room, I heard new sounds. Water sloshed, and then there was a hiss, like air escaping from a hydraulic lift. Renatè's bed was moving from side to side, up and down. Margie, the day nurse, saw me staring.

"It's called an Efficacy Bed," she explained. "Without it, we would have to rotate her periodically, which would probably be painful. This will prevent bed sores and keep her lungs clear."

Dr. Soliman, her pulmonologist, entered the room with Renatĕ's chart in hand. We exchanged polite hellos.

"There has been some improvement in her lung function and liver enzymes," he told me. "I'm going to reduce the breaths per minute that the ventilator is providing. We'll have to continue dialysis, though; her kidney function has not improved." I watched silently as he consulted with Margie before leaving the room.

Although blood was in Renatĕ's nose and mouth, it looked like she was accepting the ventilator better. She was no longer chewing on the tube. I pulled the chair next to her bed and sat holding her hand, her fingers intertwined with mine. I watched her every move, hoping for a response. If she sighed, if she moaned, if she did anything—it could have been a sign she was becoming conscious again. I wanted to be there at that moment.

Hours passed and I was stiff from sitting so long, so I got up, stretched, and walked around the room. I turned and looked down at her and noticed the blood around the ventilator tube was starting to trickle down her cheeks. At first, I thought it was coming from her cut lip, but there seemed to be too much blood. Then blood started to come out of her nose. I was about to leave to find Margie, so that she could clean her up when blood started oozing out of Renatĕ's eyes and ears, but I couldn't believe what I was seeing. I stood there with my mouth open and panicked. I stammered for a while before I was able to call out to Margie. "Please come quick! She's bleeding!"

Margie rushed into the room and when she saw Renatè, she barked at one of the other nurses to call Dr. Hartley. She asked me to leave the room as a flurry of nurses rushed in. My sister's body looked like something from a horror film. All that blood was repulsive, and yet I wanted to stay to see how they were going to stop it. This ghastly thing was happening to her and I was powerless. I reluctantly stepped out into the hallway.

When Margie called me back into the room, she explained that the doctor ordered Heparin to thin Renatè's blood and that she had a bad reaction to it. They switched her to another blood thinner, and once they cleaned Renatè up, she was resting peacefully again.

I was watching her sleep when the familiar sound of Dingo boots on linoleum interrupted my concentration. My heart jumped. There was only one person whose stride matched that cadence—my oldest brother, Cyril.

I turned to see him in the doorway. His 6-foot frame was slightly hunched over, which I assumed was caused by fatigue from the drive from Minnesota. He had a medium build and was strong, and I knew this because we usually greeted each other by wrestling. Except for a few occasions when we declared a draw, he always won. Instead of wrestling me, he gave me a big hug, and then we walked arm-in-arm over to Renatè's bedside.

As a career U. S. Navy man, I knew Cyril would approach Renatè's care with military precision, so I briefed him so that he would be prepared when it was his turn to take over the watch.

"Dr. Soliman said that she will have to continue dialysis because her kidneys are not responding," I told him.

He looked down at her quietly for several moments, then shifted his weight. "If she needs a kidney, she can have one of mine."

Immediately, I averted my eyes so that he couldn't see the tears forming. I was amazed at his candor. He made the offer so matter-of-factly as if he were saying, "I'm going to get a cup of coffee, can I get you anything?" I had never heard anyone make such a generous offer. I allowed the tears to fall freely onto the bed. If I had wiped them away, he would have known I was crying and he wouldn't have known what to do. Though Cyril commanded hundreds of men on submarines, I knew he was not equipped to deal with one emotionally charged woman.

"Here's the keys to Renatè's place," I told him, handing them to him. "You probably need to rest after that long drive." I gave him another hug. "I'll see you later."

In the days to come, Cyril and I took turns staying overnight with her. Cyril is the quintessential protective big brother. Once when I was about 9 or 10 years old, I was running down the stairs of our apartment building. I tripped and fell onto a grate at the bottom of the stairs and skinned my knee badly. Cyril found me there crying and in pain, and because he was a typical teenager, I thought he was going to tease me for being so clumsy. Instead, he lifted me and carried me all the way back up the stairs to our apartment. I'll never forget how easily that protective, big brother instinct seemed to kick in for him.

R*E*S*P*E*C*T

After Cyril left the hospital room, I resumed my position sitting at her bedside. The nurses changed shifts and now Becky was on duty.

"The daily transfusions haven't brought Renatè hemoglobin up sufficiently," Becky told me. "She's at 9 now. Dr Hartley ordered another unit of blood."

"Yesterday she was at 8," I said. "That's some improvement."

Becky smiled. "The nurses and I have been talking, and we've never seen a family so involved in their loved one's care. You must be very close."

I could feel tears welling up in the back of my eyes. "It's natural that we would look out for her," I replied. "She would do the same for any one of us. I'm just glad you don't throw us out when visiting hours are over. If we're ever in the way, let us know. We don't want to interfere with your duties."

Even though I may have questioned what the medical staff was doing at times, I did so in a tactful way. And I never challenged their competence. My parents had taught us to always be respectful to others. One occasion came to mind that was a powerful lesson in respect.

It was 1969. The sun was high in the sky and felt good against my skin. Chirping birds made the day seem even brighter. My mother, sister, and I were on a shopping trip. I was twelve, my sister ten. I was so excited to be shopping with my mother that my heart raced, and I wanted to skip instead of walk. To my mother, shopping was a sport—the thrill of the hunt. Every outing was the opportunity to discover something new.

Creating a good impression was important to my mother. Before we left, she put on the multicolored sheath she made, the one that brought her chestnut complexion to life. Her long black hair was neatly twisted in a bun at the nape of her neck and her lips and nails were colored with her favorite shade: Avon's *Wine with Everything*. Mommy's ensemble was completed with sensible pumps, the kind of shoes suitable for *power shopping*.

My sister and I were also well-dressed in matching pastel dresses. Despite our two year difference in age, Mommy insisted on dressing us like twins. At the time, it infuriated me; I wanted my own separate identity. It wasn't until I was older that I realized that she dressed us alike because she sewed all of our clothes, and it was easier for her to repeat the same pattern.

When we arrived at the shopping center, we walked across the courtyard where flowering bushes lined the sidewalks, their sweet fragrance floating in the air. In the center of the plaza, a bronze statue of a man on a horse—probably some Confederate soldier—towered over everything. Two water fountains emanated from pedestals in the corner and one fountain was labeled "Whites Only," while the other stated "Coloreds." At the time, I didn't know what the signs meant. The only frame of reference I had was the division of white and colored laundry, but that didn't make any sense in this context.

As we approached a store, an older white woman abruptly brushed past us. She acted as if we weren't even there. My face got hot. I wasn't accustomed to being treated rudely. When she placed herself in front of the doors blocking our way into the store, it struck me as strange behavior even for an old person. I looked up at my mother for some explanation.

To my surprise, my mother walked up, opened the door for the woman, and allowed her to enter the store first. My mother then put her arms around our shoulders and bent down. Her brow was furrowed and her lips were thin. I rarely saw such a serious expression on her.

"There are people who think black people are inferior to whites, even though it isn't true," she said. "When I was growing up, black people were expected to defer to whites. That woman probably thought I was obligated to open the door for her because I am black, but I wasn't obligated. I opened the door for her out of respect for her age and because that's what polite people do for one another. Sometimes you have to set pride aside in order to do the right thing."

Even at that young age, I realized the importance of the lesson she gave us. Her words made my chest swell with pride. I couldn't have been more proud to be a black person and proud to be this woman's daughter.

With this moment from our childhood in mind, I stood up and straightened the sheets around Renatè. When I saw the dry erase board on the wall, I realized I hadn't recorded her vital signs for the day. I took the journal out of my tote bag and copied the statistics from the board. I then turned back toward the bed again and stared down at Renatè.

Becky noticed how intently I was staring. "You can talk to her," Becky said. "She can hear you."

I paused at first as a jumble of words entered my mind. Then the words seem to stick in my throat. I finally exhaled and said, "I know you can beat this. Before you know it, we'll be watching *Wrestlemania*." I paused again. "I love you and I want you back. Please don't leave me here alone." I could say no more without crying, so I got up and left the room.

Daddy met me in the hallway. "What's wrong, buddy?" he asked.

"Nothing, I'm fine," I said, wiping away the tears.

"Let's go get something to eat. You'll feel better after you've eaten."

We ate in silence in the cafeteria. It occurred to me that this was the first time Daddy and I had been alone since Renatè got sick. I put on a brave face with the rest of the world, and under most circumstances, I could usually be honest with my father. But it was his little girl that lay ill, possibly dying, and I didn't want to upset him. I chose my words carefully.

"Daddy, what are we going to do if Renatè gets worse?"

"We just have to pray and trust that the Lord will eventually heal her," he replied.

"But her hemoglobin is so low."

"Didn't the doctor say there had been a slight improvement?"

"Yes, but…"

"We need to be grateful for every positive sign. Don't think about all the bad things that can happen. You'll make yourself crazy. Let's take it one step at a time."

"Yes, sir."

We returned to find Mommy in the waiting room. Gesturing to the hallway leading to Renatè's room, she said, "Angela brought her prayer circle. They're in with her now."

"What!?" I said. We had agreed as a family not to let people see her in this condition to protect her privacy. "Why did you let them in?"

Mommy stared at me blankly.

My face was hot and I thought the top of my head was about to come off. Daddy and I rushed to Renatè's room. As we entered the room, there were six people surrounding her bed. The minister stood with his hands on either side of Renatè's head, while the others were holding various parts of her body. The minister recited a verse. The circle responded, "Yes, Lord" and "Thank you, Jesus."

I can count the number of times I've seen my father really mad on one hand, and this was one of them. Through clenched teeth he said, "Please take your hands off my daughter."

"We were just praying," said the minister.

"I know—and thank you for your prayers," my father said. "But I think it would be best that you leave now."

The minister and prayer circle members looked puzzled, but they complied. After they left, I watched as Daddy visibly calmed himself with deep breaths. I understood his anger. As a Christian, he didn't object to their prayers; what he objected to was them touching his little girl. Renatè was a very private person. He knew that if she were conscious, she never would have allowed people to touch her that way.

When we returned to the waiting room, I confronted Mommy. "Why did you allow them to see her?" I asked.

"They just wanted to pray for her."

"Mommy, they had their hands all over her body. They could have exposed her to all kinds of germs."

Mommy shrugged the way she always did when she knew she couldn't win an argument.

That was the nature of the relationship I had with my mother. At times, she was obstinate and wouldn't listen to reason. It was infuriating. Other times, however, she was open, kind, and generous, and it reminded me of why I loved her so much. Life with her could be a real rollercoaster ride.

Before I said something to my mother that was disrespectful, I returned to Renatè's room and stood beside her bed.

"Your mother can be a pain in the ass," I told Renatè. "She never admits when she is wrong. If you *do* leave me alone to deal with her, I promise I will follow you into the next life and haunt you."

At that, both Becky and I started laughing.

I once looked up the definition of temperance: moderation in action, thought or feeling; restraint. It described my father perfectly. He was even-tempered, polite, and always willing to help someone. He didn't let my mother's stubbornness bother him. It was "like water on a duck's back," as he would say. I wanted to learn from Daddy's example, and tried to calm myself.

"Your father is a saint. I don't know how he puts up with Mommy." I told Renatè. "And he's such a giving soul."

DAY 4

July 16, 1997

Day – Denise/Jeremy, Night – Shirley

Weight: 82.6

I would experience a flood of the memories I shared with Renatè in the hours I spent keeping vigil at her bedside. I even confessed a secret that I had been holding onto for years.

My mother was a consummate hostess, culinary artist, creative decorator, and expert seamstress. After giving birth to two sons, she finally bore me, the daughter she had dreamed of having. I was born the day before her birthday, which she considered a dual blessing. She imagined me as someone who could be molded into a refined young lady, someone to whom she could pass on her legacy. Instead, she got an absent-minded, socially awkward child with the attention span of a gnat.

As an adolescent, my mother's constant corrections made me feel as if I couldn't do anything right. I worked hard to avoid her criticism. I confessed to Renatè about the time I messed up Mommy's legendary crescent rolls, those heavenly crescent rolls that could melt in your mouth. The preparation process was so involved that it took two days. On the first day, Mommy boiled the potatoes, mixed the batter, kneaded the dough, and stored it in the refrigerator. On the second day, she rolled out the dough, shaped the crescent rolls, covered them in plastic wrap, and set them on the stove to rise. I was downstairs sewing and intently involved in my work, when Mommy stood at the top of the stairs and yelled down to me, "When you hear the timer go off, put the rolls in the oven and reset the timer for fifteen minutes." I was furious because I was busy, while Renatè wasn't doing anything. I couldn't understand why our mother always relied on me to do everything.

The timer buzzed and I ran up to the kitchen, taking the stairs two at a time. I shoved the tray into the oven, reset the timer, and then returned to my project. Fifteen minutes passed and the timer buzzed again. This time I mounted the stairs while cursing under my breath. I pulled out the tray and placed it on top of the stove.

Something didn't seem right. The rolls looked glazed on top. I knew my mother had brushed them with butter, but that was to help them brown. These were actually too shiny. I noticed a stiff ridge around the edge of the pan, and that's when it hit me. In my haste to get back to my project, I hadn't removed the plastic wrap which now stuck to the top of the rolls.

"Oh, shit," I said. After all my mother's hard work, the rolls were ruined. Or were they? I removed the plastic around the edge of the pan and stood back. The shine actually made the rolls look more enticing. Then I thought, "Can I risk my family getting sick from eating plastic to avoid my mother going ballistic?" It took me a New York minute to decide. I arranged the rolls in a breadbasket and put them on the table.

Later, as my family sat at the table, as we all passed the food around, I watched each person take a roll from the basket. My heart was pounding so hard I thought it might be visible. I hung my head and braced myself for the complaints, but instead, my mother got the usual compliments. However, I wasn't out of the woods yet. After dinner, I carefully observed everyone, becoming relieved when I saw that no one had gotten sick. The potential for my mother's disapproval had such a hold on me that, even as an adult, I had never told her that story.

It felt so good finally to be able to tell someone—even if she was unconscious.

Ever since Becky told me Renatè could hear me, I continued to talk to her. I hoped that something would trigger a response from her, even if it was only her waking up to tell me, "Shut the fuck up!" One of the stories I recounted for her was about how Mommy and I used to play fashion police.

Mommy and I loved to people watch and we saw ourselves as self-appointed fashion police. We had developed non-verbal ways of getting each other's attention so we could be as discreet as possible. Once, in the late 1990's, we were shopping at the Post Exchange, which was the U. S. Army's version of Macy's, only with ammo. It was the beginning of summer, the season most fraught with fashion infractions. A woman walked by us in a lemon-yellow and white striped top, her belly fat rolling over the top of her matching lemon yellow polyester slacks. "Someone needs to tell that woman horizontal stripes are not her friend," Mommy whispered to me. "And who the hell wears yellow anyway?"

We cruised over to the lingerie section and I spied a woman in a bright orange, racer-back tank top, her black bra straps clearly visible.

"Don't women even try to conceal their bra straps anymore?" I whispered. "You think if I grabbed one of those strapless bras off the wall and tossed it into her basket, she'd get the hint?" We both giggled.

We continued to peruse the clothing racks when I signaled Mommy to check out a woman in Capri pants that were stretched to the limit.

"She needs to go up a few sizes on those pants," I whispered.

"Her butt looks like ten pounds of flour in a one pound sack," Mommy added.

At the perfume counter, we saw a teenage girl waiting in a pink sundress. It was flattering on her petite frame, but so lightweight that you could see her panties. Mommy grabbed my arm and looked me right in the eyes.

"No matter how hot it is, you always wear a slip."

Standing in the checkout line, I nudged Mommy and averted my eyes to the feet of the woman in front of us. She was wearing sandals that looked to be a size too small, apparent by her toes curling over the front edge. The beginning of summer must have caught her off-guard, because she clearly hadn't taken time to get a pedicure. After the woman paid for her purchase and walked away, Mommy leaned in to me and said, "Didn't you know, crusty heels and troll toes are in this season?"

Mommy and I enjoyed countless outings like that. Mommy could be lighthearted and fun-loving, but she also had another side that was cynical and petty. She had a sharp sarcastic wit that was immensely entertaining—as long as she was laughing *with* you and not *at* you. For most of my life, my mother remained an enigma, as unique as her name: Abiatha (ä - bī ´- ä – thä).

ABIATHA'S WAY

My mother was a caring, compassionate person who volunteered thousands of hours to community organizations and her church. When a neighbor lost her hair to chemotherapy, my mother bought her scarves and turbans in assorted colors so that she wouldn't be embarrassed to go out in public. But for all my mother's charismatic qualities, she also had a razor sharp tongue. I don't think she knew how damaging her words could be. At age thirteen, preparing nightly meals for my family was one of my primary chores. One evening, I turned the corner to the kitchen and the acrid smell of burned spaghetti sauce filled my nostrils. My heart sank; my mother would be furious. I threw open the window, then I transferred the sauce to another pot, peeled and cubed two potatoes, and dropped them into the sauce. As they simmered, the potatoes absorbed the burned flavor. Mommy walked in and shook her head at me. "You ain't worth a dime," she murmured, and then she turned and walked out. Her words sliced through me like a serrated knife.

Looking back, I realize that a lifetime of self-doubt is rooted in encounters like that. I know Mommy loved me and wanted me to be at my best, and I can now understand that she intended her criticism to make me strive to do better. Instead, it eroded my self-esteem. It would be years before I could acknowledge my self-worth.

My mother was raised on a farm in Arkansas during the Depression. Her parents had very little money and instilled in her the belief that success in life required hard work and dedication. At the same time, they taught her that pride and vanities were sins. She taught these same values to her children.

Pleasing my mother was an almost impossible task. While she acknowledged that I was a straight-A student, she didn't treat it as an achievement. Instead, she focused on areas where I was weak, such as my domestic chores. If I sewed a garment, she always found my mistakes. If I cooked a meal, it was too salty or not salty enough. If I cleaned the house, she showed me where I missed a spot.

Despite the constant criticism, my childhood was actually happy. My parents created a loving, comfortable home for my brothers, sister, and me. Because of their experience of growing up on a farm with few amenities, they found it all the more important to provide a better life for their children. They also made sure we weren't narrow-minded. My father was a career U.S. Army soldier. When we were stationed in Germany, he would sometimes take leave so that we could travel across Europe. By the time I was eleven, I had already been to five countries.

However, my father's U.S. Army salary was limited. It was my mother, a master at stretching a dollar, who found a way for us to live a middle-class lifestyle. She was as resourceful as she was talented, and as her first-born daughter, I was the one she hoped would inherit her homemaking skills. The problem was that I was an absent-minded, socially awkward child who had difficulty focusing. Maybe I had Attention Deficit Disorder, but there was no such diagnosis back then. Whatever the cause, I knew from Mommy's reaction to me that I was a disappointment. I remember once going on a school field trip to the Frankfurt Zoo in Germany, and accidentally throwing away my new Barbie wallet with my lunch bag.

"How could you be so careless?" my mother asked when I got home. "Money doesn't grow on trees." She would recall that story, sharing it with others even after I'd become an adult. She seemed to take pleasure in pointing out my faults to friends and family.

I was in awe of my mother's talents and wanted desperately to be like her. Somehow, she seemed to just know things. One Christmas, I decided to paint a scene on our front window. The theme was children of the world. When it came time to paint the faces, I needed shades of brown. I knew my primary and secondary colors, but I didn't know how to mix brown paint.

My mother was sitting at the dining room table and gossiping with a friend. I politely interrupted, explained my dilemma, and asked her to take me to the store. She turned to me and without hesitation said, "Just mix green with pink." That sounded ridiculous, and I thought she was just feeding me any old answer in order to get rid of me. But I did as she suggested and was surprised when it worked. My mother had never taken an art class in her life; she was just naturally creative.

As far back as I could remember, Mommy was volunteering for one organization or another. Today she would be considered a stay-at-home-mom, though she didn't spend all her time at home. When we were young, she worked with the American Red Cross and the USO. She was also a den mother for my brothers' Boy Scout troop.

As we got older, Mommy turned her attention to community organizations. She held several offices in the Disabled American Veterans Auxiliary, where they ultimately elected her Commander for the State of Kansas. She was also active with Lion's Club International and received the Melvin Johnson Award, the highest honor bestowed on a member.

When our classroom teachers needed room mothers, Mommy always volunteered. For my brothers, sister and me, it was a double-edged sword. On one edge, we knew we had to be on our best behavior. On the other, we felt such pride when she provided treats for our holiday parties. Other moms brought Tootsie Pops or Sugar Daddies, but our mother made elaborately decorated cupcakes and cookies. She also planned extraordinary birthday celebrations. I have pictures of us—girls in frilly dresses and boys in suits and ties—standing around a festive table for my sister's birthday. Mommy prided herself on creating unique cakes. My favorites were the carousels, which was when she would surround the cake with animal cookies painted with icing and use licorice as the poles.

Despite what I saw as my limitations, I never ceased trying to be a good chef. There was the time I wanted to impress a friend my brother had brought home from college, and so I prepared a meal of comfort foods I knew he would appreciate. To top it off, I decided to make Baked Alaska.

My chicken was fried to a golden brown crisp, the potatoes were whipped light and fluffy, and the macaroni and cheese had just the right amount of cheddar. I was feeling good about my meal, until I pulled the dessert out of the oven. This was when I learned a cardinal rule of entertaining: *never* try a new recipe. My Baked Alaska should have been named Baked Washington because it looked like Mount St. Helens after the eruption. There was no point dwelling on the failure, so I stashed the dish in the refrigerator and focused on finishing the rest of the meal.

As we ate, I soaked in all the smiling faces around the table. I was proud that everyone enjoyed my dinner, but that pride was short lived. At the end of the meal, my mother turned to my brother's friend and said, "I'm sorry, but Cynthia wasn't able to prepare a proper dessert, so we only have vanilla ice cream to offer you."

Later that evening, I joined my father, who was tucked away in his recliner chewing on something. My father has maintained a 32-inch waistline his entire adult life despite constantly eating.

"What's that you have there?" I asked.

"Don't know," he said. "Found it in the fridge." On closer inspection, I realized it was my Baked Alaska. "Tastes pretty good," he added.

I bent down and kissed the top of his head.

"What's that for?" he asked.

"For being you."

He smiled and went back to eating.

In the days that followed, my father ate every spoonful of my disaster. At that time in my life, I may have had a mother who was my worst critic, but I fortunately also had a father who was my biggest fan.

Furthermore, Mommy was very specific about how we completed our chores. There was only one way to fold laundry, iron a shirt, hang clothes on the line, cut up a chicken—and that was Abiatha's way. Towels had to be folded lengthwise first, with the seams to the inside, then crosswise and stacked with the folded edge facing forward. Shirt collars and back yolks were ironed first, then the front, back, and finally the sleeves. Clothes that were alike were hung on the line together in ascending order of size, from underwear to sheets. We had the most organized clothesline in the neighborhood.

Occasionally, I would deviate from her system, just to get under her skin. But in the end, I knew she'd make me go back and do it the 'right' way. (When I recently saw towels rolled into bundles in my sister's linen closet, I knew that she had escaped the conditioning. I, on the other hand, am still compelled to fold them Abiatha's way.)

For years, I thought Mommy's organized, almost compulsive behavior was the result of her being born under the astrological sign of Virgo. It was only recently that I realized how those qualities grew from necessity. Daddy was away on duty sometimes months at a time, which meant my mother was often a single parent. With four small children, she had to have systems in order to maintain a stable household. By involving me with basic chores, she taught me how to be thorough, analytical, and accountable, all qualities that would become important to me later in my career as an event manager.

After I left home for college, it was easier for me to acknowledge my strengths. I learned that my talents weren't inferior to my mother's, they were simply different. I wasn't as focused as she was on symmetry and order. I liked breaking the rules, and once I no longer had her watching over my shoulder, I was able to prepare meals without burning anything.

DAY 5

July 17, 1997

Day – Jeremy/Denise, Night – Jack

Weight: 79

I had been sitting with Renatè for hours and needed a break. "I think I'll stretch my legs and walk down to the cafeteria," I said to the night nurse, Denise. "Would you like anything?"

"No, thanks."

The rest of the hospital wasn't as cold as the ICU. I could feel my joints loosening up as I walked to the cafeteria and back. When I returned, there were people in the waiting room with Mommy and Daddy. They were acquaintances from some of the many church and civic organizations for which my parents volunteered. My parents traveled extensively for organizational functions and had friends in towns dotted across the state.

Word of Renatè's illness spread quickly and people came to offer their support. Previously, Renatè worked for St. Vincent Hospital as Environmental Services Manager, so many of her staff and co-workers also came by to see how she was doing. I found it hard to sit and visit with people. I couldn't feign agreement with their platitudes.

"This is God's will."

"God won't put more on you than you can handle."

"God has a plan. It's not our place to question him."

It was as if they were trying to prepare us for the worst. I was a Christian, but I felt guilty because I didn't want to hear any of that crap.

I sat with my parents' visitors for a while before excusing myself. I was anxious to be back in the room with Renatè. In her room, I could pretend we were just hanging out. I played this game with myself to deal with the rollercoaster of emotions. I could go from hopeful to sad to angry to fearful in a matter of minutes depending on what incident was next. I had been so naïve, thinking that Renatè would always recover from every SCA crisis. As I sat holding her hand and watching her chest rise and fall with the ventilator, it was as if rose-colored glasses had been removed from my eyes. Now I could see how the real world operates. I could see that the real world is not fair.

I was taught that if you work hard, help others in need, and treat people with respect, good things would come to you. But no one bothered to mention, "Oh, and by the way, a loved one may be taken from you when you least expect it. And you'll be left feeling like someone reached into your chest with their bare hands and ripped your heart out."

As I pondered this tragic twist of fate, Cyril appeared in the doorway. His presence had been a blessing. I could take a break from the tedium of spending hour after hour at my sister's bedside.

"How's she doing?" he asked.

"She's been resting quietly. Her hemoglobin is up a notch, but she still has a long way to go. Suddenly remembering that Cyril was the math whiz in our family, I handed him my journal. "They weigh her in kilograms; can you convert these figures for me?"

He scribbled on the journal for a few moments, and then looked up at me.

"What?" I asked.

"According to my calculations, she's lost thirty five pounds since she's been here."

I stared at him in disbelief. "That can't be right."

"Let me check." He scribbled again. "I'm afraid it's true." He paused. "Maybe it's the dialysis. It draws a lot of fluid out of the body."

"You're right, that's it." I didn't want to believe that anything more sinister was happening. With so much going on, I hadn't noticed the weight loss, though I noticed that her cheekbones had become more pronounced.

"I know that trying to sleep is hard, but go home and try to rest," Cyril said.

When I got home, I couldn't relax. Everything in Renatè's apartment was a reminder of the unique and vivacious person that she is.

I sat down on the sofa, ready to stretch out for the night. I looked around the living room and saw a picture of Renatè with a Bahaman police officer. Renatè was always impressed by men in uniform. Wherever she traveled, she always took a picture with a policeman, who was usually flattered and accommodating. There was also a picture of the two of us sitting on high-back wicker chairs with our legs crossed in the Bahamas. We looked majestic. Hours after that picture was taken, we were listening to a sales pitch.

In exchange for listening to a presentation on timeshares, we received a free cruise to the Bahamas with hotel accommodations. We just wanted the free trip and had zero interest in a timeshare, which seemed like a fair trade since we both were overdue for a break from work.

On our way to the sales office, we walked past a series of *Architectural Digest*-quality townhomes surrounding a manmade lake. The property was landscaped with lush tropical flowering bushes, mostly fuchsia and red bougainvillea. The sun was high, feeling more intense against my skin than the California sun I was used to, and the sky was crystal blue with wisps of white scattered clouds.

We entered an office that had several desks where salespeople were meeting with prospective clients. We felt special, because we were ushered into a private office where we met a pleasant man named Richard. He had a brilliant smile and the kind of personality that made you feel at ease. His complexion was rich and dark, reminiscent of Sidney Poitier.

Richard explained the concept of timeshares, telling us that we would be purchasing property which we'd have access to for one week each year. "We have a plan that will give you deluxe accommodations for just $400 a month," he said, as he showed us pictures of exquisitely furnished townhomes.

Renatè and I both laughed.

"They would only be $200 each," he added quickly.

"That's still more than I'm willing to spend," Renatè replied.

"Well, how much are you willing to spend?"

"Nothing," I said. "We can't always spend vacations together. It took us six months to schedule this trip. I'll admit that you have nice properties."

"But we will have to pass," Renatè chimed in without missing a beat.

With that, we left the office with our sales resistance intact. I hated to disappoint Richard. He was extremely professional and had a great sales pitch, but in hindsight, it was a good thing we didn't buy a timeshare, because we would never have been able to return.

After thinking about that memory from our trip, I decided that the next day, I would take several pictures to her hospital room. I wanted the nurses to see her as a complete person and not just as a patient. They only see people at their worst, but I wanted them to know that she had a happy life to come back to. When Renatè woke up, I wanted her to see pictures of us in happier times so that she would know that this was just a temporary situation and that when she was well, we would travel again.

Finally, my eyes came to a large painting on the wall that her former boyfriend had given her. In the portrait, Renatè wore a black dress with a gold satin collar that circled her décolletage. She was glancing over her right shoulder, her look pensive, but pleasant. She may have had Daddy's eyes, but her complexion and high cheekbones were definitely Mommy's. The painting reminded me of photos of Mommy from when she was younger, and my sister had the same grace, elegance. The artist had completely captured Renatè's essence.

My eyes then became transfixed, as if Renatè's spirit was in the room with me. I felt a dull pain in my chest when I remembered why she was not physically there, and couldn't look at the portrait any longer. I took it down and faced it toward the wall, then curled up on the sofa and pulled the quilt over me. A few tears rolled down my cheek. Those few were all I would allow. Renatè was coming home someday. I wouldn't allow myself to think otherwise.

DAY 6

July 18, 1997

Day – Denise/Jeremy, Night – Tammy

Weight: 82.9

The next morning, I drove Renatè's Renault to the hospital. The radio was on, but I hadn't really been listening until a song came on that caught my attention. In the refrain, the artist Trisha Yearwood sang,

How do I live without you?

Yearwood repeated the refrain several times and I noticed my hands started to shake on the steering wheel, so I pulled over to the side of the road. My whole body shuddered. I couldn't hold back any longer. All of the effort to remain brave for Renatè and my family was gone. The quiet voice inside me that had been telling me everything was going to be okay was now silent as my fear of losing her took over. A wretched pain gripped me. I could feel it in every joint of my body. For the first time, I admitted to myself that there was a possibility that she could die. I realized that just like the Tricia Yearwood song lyrics, I wouldn't know how to live without her. I sobbed uncontrollably.

When I finished crying, I wiped my eyes and tried to brush the lint of the now shredded tissue from my face. I looked at myself in the rearview mirror and into my bloodshot eyes, knowing that there would be no hiding my feelings that day. I continued on to the hospital.

I entered Renatè's room and set my tote bag on the chair as always, but when I turned toward the bed I had to take a step backwards. Renatè's eyes were open. There was no fanfare. The heavens didn't open up, and there was no angelic choir singing "Hallelujah!" Nonetheless, it was a miracle. When her gaze met mine, she frowned.

"Welcome back, stranger," I told Renatè. "You had a really bad Sickle Cell crisis, and you're in the hospital." I didn't want to tell her more than that. To tell her about her liver, lung, and kidney failure at that point would only scare her. "You are in good hands. A team of specialists is taking care of you."

She tried to talk, but the ventilator prevented her from speaking. She reached up and pulled at the tube, trying to remove it. I grabbed her hand.

"No, Renatè, the ventilator is helping you breathe. Until your lungs are strong enough, you'll need it."

She frowned and moved her lips around the tube.

"I'm sorry, I don't understand what you're trying to say. Are you in pain?"

She quickly shook her head no and tried moving her lips again. Still unable to understand, I could only shrug my shoulders. She raised her right hand and moved her wrist as if she were writing in the air.

"You want to write?"

She nodded. I rummaged through my tote bag and gave her a notepad and pen. With pen in hand, she began marking the page, and when she was through, she presented it to me with pride. All that was on the paper was a series of scribbles—no letters, no words. The morphine must have affected her cognition and coordination.

Once more, I apologized. "I can't understand your writing," I said.

She balled up her fists and pounded the bed.

"Calm down, don't get upset. I'll figure out something, but you need to rest now."

Her eyelids fluttered softly as if she was fighting sleep, but finally, she gave in. I quietly took the photos out of my tote bag, strategically placed them where Renatè would see them, and slumped into the chair. It was as if every muscle in my body that had been tight for so long could now relax, so I took advantage of the opportunity to get some long overdue sleep myself.

When I awoke, I immediately checked to see if her eyes were still open. Once I saw that they were, I noticed a man stood reviewing Renatè's chart in the corner of the room. He didn't look like the other doctors that tended to her, and wasn't even wearing a lab coat. He introduced himself as Dr. Brown, the senior physician in charge of her overall care.

"None of her doctors can determine why so many of her systems were affected," he said. "It's uncharacteristic for SCA to affect the liver, lungs, kidneys, and brain at the same time."

"The brain?" I asked. "What do you mean?" This was the first time anyone mentioned anything about her brain being affected.

"Renatè was in a coma for the last 4 days," he replied.

The word coma stunned me. In an instant, I felt like a fog surrounded me as I vaguely heard the doctor continuing to talk in the background. Everything I knew about comas came from television. People would be in comas for months, years. Some never recovered. To learn that Renatè had been comatose was shocking to me, and I realized how much the Lord has a way of protecting us. Had I spent the past week knowing she was in a coma, I don't know if I could have coped.

I came out of the fog just as Dr. Brown was saying, "She is very fortunate to have survived all of that."

I looked down at Renatè to see her mouth moving again. I could see in her eyes how determined she was determined to talk to me.

"Dr. Brown, she keeps trying to talk to me, but I don't understand her. She's concentrating so hard and I don't want to wear her out."

"You're right, it would be best to wait until she's stronger." He excused himself and walked out of the room, still reading her chart.

The rest of the day, I tried to keep Renatè calm. I reminded her that the doctor said she needed her rest, but she wouldn't give up trying to talk to me. Finally, I agreed to allow her to tell me one word.

"Let's try using the alphabet. Hold my hand and I will call out the letters of the alphabet. When I get to the letter you want, squeeze my hand."

Her face relaxed. I was relieved to see that she agreed.

I started calling off the alphabet. "A – B – C – D..."

On the letter D, she squeezed my hand. I was thrilled! Now we could finally communicate. I continued with my alphabet method. I called out, "A – B – C – D – E." On the letter E, she squeezed my hand again. Her eyelids fluttered. She slowly turned her head away from me. The morphine made it hard for her to stay focused.

"Maybe you should rest and we'll try again later."

"No," she mouthed. "Please."

"Okay, we'll finish, but then you have to promise me you'll rest."

Lethargically, she drew a cross on her heart with her finger. She selected the letter "A" to begin again, then "T" and finally "H." I repeated the letters aloud, but it wasn't until I wrote them on the note pad that I realized what she had spelled: "DEATH."

Panic washed over me. The notebook and pen fell out of my hand and onto the bed as I started to hyperventilate. I hung on to the bed railing to steady myself. Finally, I composed myself, well enough to speak.

"You're not going to die. You don't remember, but you have been through the worst of this crisis. You're better now. This is not like any other time when you've been sick. It may take a long time for you to fully recover, but you *will* recover." The words were coming out of my mouth so quickly that I must have sounded like an old tape recorder on fast-forward.

I had to leave the room because I knew I was going to cry. In the hall, I kept wondering whether she was asking a question or making a statement. Her eyes had been wide, but her face had no expression. She had suffered excruciating pain from SCA for almost 40 years. Did being critically ill make her want to give up? Was she telling me that she'd rather die than be on a ventilator? Moreover, was I prepared to let her go if that was her decision?

I found Cyril in the cafeteria and hurried over to him. "I was trying to communicate with Renatè, and she spelled out the word 'death,'" I said. "Do you think that means she wants to die?"

He shook his head and placed a calming hand on my shoulder. "No, she must be thinking the worst might happen because we're all here. She's surprised to see us—especially me. Since we haven't been in contact otherwise, it must be a shock to see me." Cyril told me exactly what I needed to hear at that moment regardless of whether it was true or not. He said what he knew would calm me down. He was good at that.

Cyril's presence only made me miss my other brother Curtis that much more. If he knew about Renatè's condition, he would have wanted to be there. Yet, all of the phone numbers we had for him were disconnected.

Several years earlier, and much to my parents' dismay, Curtis dropped out of law school. In lieu of getting what my parents would call a "real job"—their term for something professional—he was waiting tables in high-end restaurants in Kansas City. He worked hard, but he played harder. Curtis loved to party. My parents didn't approve of his lifestyle which drove a wedge between them. I never passed judgment on him and we remained close, but sometimes months would pass before I would hear from him. Even then, it was usually because he wanted to borrow money. His absence at that critical time weighed heavy on my heart, and I couldn't help but resent him for not staying in touch with the family.

DAY 7

July 19, 1997

Day - Denise/Jeremy, Night – Shirley

Weight: 82.5

Renatè spit up blood for most of the day. I could tell by her wide-eyed expression that it was freaking her out. When she coughed, her nose would bleed. There was so much blood everywhere that it was hard for the nurses to keep her dressings clean. Watching her spit up blood was like something from a horror movie. The nurses gave her platelets and another unit to help her blood coagulate, and as they busily went about their duties, I was constantly moving around to stay out of their way. I just wanted to make sure that Renatè could always see me.

The nurses were busy changing her dressings, checking her vital signs and administering medications, buzzing in and out of the room like bees. I felt so useless, but all I could do was try to keep Renatè's spirits up.

In between dancing around the nurses, I talked to Renatè about some of the stunts we pulled over the years, though some of which were entirely my own doing. A favorite of mine was closet shopping. My mother had an enviable sense of style. She bought classic clothing with the best quality that she could afford, and because she was such a savvy shopper, people marveled at how well she dressed. When I was in college, I lived close enough to go home on weekends. The benefit was that I got free laundry service, and I could also engage in an enterprise I liked to call closet shopping.

Closet shopping was best accomplished when Mommy was out doing errands, and it had many advantages. Mommy had three closets so she rarely noticed what was missing, and because she and I wore the same size, there was a wide selection from which to choose. I was also smart enough not to wear my ill-gotten gains in her presence.

On one occasion, she left for the grocery store, and I knew it would be at least a 2-hour trip because she was obsessed with cruising every aisle. Once I heard her car pull away, I got started in the master bedroom, where her most recent acquisitions were.

I threw open her closet door and revealed what resembled a crayon's box of colors. Though it was neatly organized, I found it overwhelming. I decided to start at one end and work my way across the rack, focusing on certain kinds of garments. Suits, for example, would come in handy since I was graduating soon, so I pulled out several and laid them on the bed.

The emerald one had a shawl collar with black piping and welt pockets, but it looked too 'lunch with the ladies,' so it went back in the closet. The sapphire one had a pencil skirt with kick pleat that was cute, but skirts required pantyhose, which equaled torture to me, so it went back in the closet. The ruby one had so many gold buttons, I felt like I should salute it. It went back in the closet. The amethyst one had a medium width collar instead of the wide 1980's look that was prevalent at the time. It would be fashionable for years, while the slacks were exactly the right length—in other words, *perfect*.

Larceny aside, part of the reason I enjoyed raiding Mommy's closet was that I could smell her signature fragrance, Estee' Lauder Private Collection, on her clothes. I only associated that sweet, exotic scent with her, and wearing Mommy's clothes made me feel like she was always with me.

For some reason, I didn't hear the garage door open. I didn't hear her open the back door, either. However, I did hear Mommy drop her keys on the dining room table. I flew into my bedroom, changed clothes in seconds, and stashed the suit in my luggage.

She greeted me in the hallway. "Where's your daddy?" she asked.

"He's downstairs watching TV." I tried to speak evenly despite the fact that my heart was pounding and I was out of breath. Inside, I smiled—another mission accomplished.

The rest of the weekend went as usual; I shopped with Mommy and fixed cars with Daddy. On Sunday, I went into my bedroom to finish packing and found a box next to my suitcase. I lifted the lid to see a pair of amethyst pumps inside. I stood there with my mouth open.

Mommy passed by my bedroom doorway. "You might as well have the whole ensemble," she said.

Like the warm scent of Estee' Lauder on her clothes, I was bathed in her generosity.

Telling Renatè that story broke up some of the tension that had been building throughout the day as the nurses struggled to keep her dressings dry. Finally, around 5 o'clock, Renatè stopped spitting up blood, they got her cleaned up and she was able to rest. I had thought that since she was more alert, I could read her get well cards to her that day. I even brought her Tickle-Me-Elmo doll from home, knowing how his incessant giggling always cheered her up. But she was too preoccupied for any of that. In my journal that day, I wrote "Today is a day I'd like to forget. I hope Renatè doesn't remember it either."

This would be my last full day with her. It broke my heart to think about leaving, but I'd only made my flight reservation for one week. My employer understood my last-minute departure, but I had to get back to cover events that were scheduled. By the end of the day, I was worn out just from watching Renatè. I went home and collapsed onto the sofa.

DAY 8

July 19, 1997

Day – Jeremy/Denise, Night – Shirley

Weight: 82.5

When I arrived at the hospital the next day, Cyril pulled me aside in the hallway. "Dr. Hartley said she has blood in her lungs and stomach," he said. "They can't tell if it is from her nose bleeding or something else. But the number one concern is the infection in her colon. Even her kidneys have become a secondary concern. As long as there is an infection, the other organs won't function properly. They called in Dr. Renyard and he ordered a CAT scan."

I told Cyril how much I had been dreading this day, but he told me not to worry. He, Mommy and Daddy would look after her.

I took a deep breath and moved over to the bed to talk to Renatè. She looked up at me wide-eyed. "I have to go back to California," I told her. "They need me at work, but I'll be calling to check on you. You be sure to do what the doctors tell you so you can get better soon." I could feel the back of my eyes burning but I didn't want to cry. "I'll be returning in a few weeks and I want to see you walk out of here."

Before I left, I helped her sit up in bed so I could give her a hug. Her body seemed delicate, frail. She barely lifted her arms to encircle me, but I held her tightly.

Over the coming weeks, my family reported to me that Renatè's liver enzymes improved, her hemoglobin went up to 11, her kidney function returned, and the doctors found the right combination of antibiotics to fight off the infection. In order for her to be taken off the ventilator, though, they had to be convinced her lungs were strong enough for her to breathe on her own.

To test her lungs, they did a procedure called blowback. Once before I left, the nurse allowed me to stay in the room during the procedure because Renatè was much calmer when I was around. Unfortunately, I was sorry that I stayed. The procedure involved inserting a tube down her throat to measure her lung function. While they inserted the tube, they shut off her airway for almost a minute. A minute is a long time to go without air. I've since tried holding my breath for that long and had a hard time doing it. The fear in Renatè's eyes when they did the procedure spoke volumes. They repeated the procedure several times over the course of several weeks and finally after a month on the ventilator, she passed her test.

As I promised, I dutifully called every day, but it was hard being so far away. Two weeks after I left, she was stronger, but still had a while to go before she would be fully recovered.

"So how's our patient today?" I asked Mommy.

"She's doing well. They had her up and she walked in the hall today. Here, I'll let her tell you."

Excited, I waited until I heard Renatè's breathing on the other end of the line. "Hey," I said, "how you doin'?"

"Hangin' tough, hangin' tough," she said, her voice soft as a kitten's breath.

"Heard you took a trip down the hall."

"Yeah, wore my ass out."

"You'll get better at it. How's the appetite?" I asked. Whenever Renatè was sick growing up, we had problems getting her to eat.

"So, so."

"Is the food any good?"

"It's all right. I'm just not hungry."

"Well, you need to eat to get your strength back."

"I know. They're talking about releasing me from the hospital this week. They want me to go to a rehab center for a few weeks. When are you coming back?"

"Two weeks from Saturday."

"Cool."

Saturday came and I couldn't have been more excited. The rehab facility was nice, its traditional furnishings, plants, and over-stuffed chairs giving it a warm homey atmosphere.

I entered Renatè's room. She was fully dressed and sitting on the edge of her bed. It was great to see her in something other than a flimsy hospital gown. Mommy was sitting in a chair beside the bed, while Daddy stood looking out the window. I rushed over and gave them each a hug.

"I'm so glad you're here," Renatè said. "Now I can bust out of this place."

"Yeah, Mommy said you want to walk AMA." AMA meant against medical advice. And though I knew my sister was determined I said,

"This is a great place. Don't you want to stay and make sure you're stronger?"

Tears welled up in her eyes and she started to sob. "I want to go home. I want to sleep in my own bed. I don't need nurses anymore."

I was nervous about her going home so soon. She wasn't strong enough to resume her normal routine. What if she had a relapse? Still, I knew her well enough to know she was determined. Once her mind was made up, there was no changing it.

"Okay, okay." I rubbed her back as she leaned against me. "We'll get you home."

Since she was leaving AMA, we didn't have to wait for paperwork to be filled out. I packed her belongings into a tote bag and called for a wheelchair. She shuffled her feet toward the chair like the little old man Tim Conway used to portray on the *Carol Burnett Show*, and I couldn't resist the temptation to tease her so I mimicked her steps behind her.

"Bite me," she said. Once she sat in the chair, she pointed toward the door. "Let's roll, troll!"

Daddy brought the car around to the front door. When I wheeled her out into the blazing hot Kansas sun, I felt my chest expand twice its size. My heart was full. Our bond as a family had been strengthened by the near tragedy, our lives forever changed. We had a renewed respect for how precious we all were to each other.

BEYOND SADNESS

The crisis was over. In the coming months, Renatè recovered and didn't seem to have suffered any permanent damage from the Sickle Cell Anemia. It was time for me to return to the tedium of everyday life. I threw myself into my work as an events manager, filling my days by meeting with clients, coordinating event details, and marketing projects for more work. I was also responsible for advancing performances for the main theater.

Working twelve to fourteen hour days, six days a week advancing performances for the main theater took its toll on me. I contacted road managers and agents to review their artists' needs for ground transportation, backstage catering, security, and merchandising. Over the years, I've been privileged to have been a part of presenting artists like Frank Sinatra, Penn and Teller, Baryshnikov, The Four Tops, Joan Rivers, Alvin Ailey American Dance Theater and Whitney Houston.

On my days off, I was so exhausted I had to force myself to get out of bed. I tried to stay connected to friends, but it took great effort to stay active outside of work when all I wanted to do was sleep. Still, I was desperate to try to maintain the semblance of a normal life. One Saturday, I had been invited to a Creative Memories group where people gather together to work on their scrapbooks. I love making scrapbooks and didn't want to miss the opportunity to work on my latest one about our family vacation in Puerto Vallarta, Mexico. The fact that it was one year after Renatě's illness made it a special vacation. But when I awoke that morning I realized I had slept through the alarm. I only had forty minutes to shower, dress and drive to a Days Inn twenty miles away.

I quickly ran through the shower, dried off, pulled on a t-shirt and a pair of jeans that I had thrown over the banister after the last time I wore them, and rushed out the door. I arrived at the hotel a half hour late. I grabbed my gear and headed for the room the group had reserved. On the way to the room, I passed two Asian men. One of them was pointing at me. As a black woman living in Orange County California, I am accustomed to being stared at, so I just ignored them.

Once in the room, I located my friends. Thankfully they had saved a space for me at their table. I removed my supplies from my bag and shoved it under the table. As I looked down, I saw something pastel peeking from below the leg of my jeans. On closer inspection I realized it was a pair of panties. Apparently, the last time I wore the jeans, I left the panties inside.

I was mortified. How could I not have realized I was dragging a pair of panties behind me? I looked around the room. There was no way I would be able to slip out to the bathroom without the panties falling completely out. Using the tablecloth as a shield, I pulled the panties out of my jeans leg and tossed them further under the table. Then I sent up a prayer hoping that no one would look under the table. They didn't.

This incident typified my world at the time. I was stumbling through life trying to get my act together; always feeling as though I were two steps behind the rest of the world. I couldn't escape the feeling that at any moment something bad was going to happen. I had what I called "grey days" where I went about my everyday tasks in a fog. I felt disconnected from everything. Things that normally brought me joy—like trying new foods, for example—no longer had appeal.

After Renatè's illness, I felt a deep sense of loss. This went on for about seven years. I did not lose my sister, and she is still a big part of my life, but the day she fell silent—slipped into a coma—the logical world I thought I lived in ceased to exist. Renatè had done nothing to deserve her circumstances, so why had it happened? It made me question my faith and the fairness of life. Ultimately, I would learn the source of my pessimism. I came to realize that I was battling an insidious disease of my own.

One day as I was filling out a form, my mind went blank when I came to the space for my social security number. I couldn't believe it. How could I forget my social security number? My heart started racing, as my mind zipped through all the scenarios and consequences of forgetting such an important detail. Social security numbers are the key to our identity. For security reasons, I don't have the number written down anywhere, so I had no place to check for it. My palms were sweating, I couldn't catch my breath and I was getting lightheaded. I was now in full panic mode.

At the earliest opportunity, I made an appointment with Dr. Ryan, who had been my general practitioner for over ten years. I liked her because she really listened. She understood me and knew my family's experience with SCA, so I didn't have to explain my situation every time I visited her. I also appreciated that she never seemed to be rushing to get to the next patient the way some doctors do.

Dr. Ryan, I imagined, was close to my age, which at the time would have been early 40's. She had curly brown hair and her round glasses rested on rosy cheeks. She greeted me with her customary broad smile.

"So what brings you to see me today, my dear?"

"I think I have Alzheimer's disease," I said.

She frowned. "What makes you say that?"

"I can never find my keys when I need them and the other day I couldn't remember my social security number."

Dr. Ryan looked at me earnestly. "I know that the progression of your father's Alzheimer's disease is weighing heavy on your mind. Yes, Alzheimer's disease is hereditary, but no, you don't have it."

"How can you tell?"

"There's a big difference between losing your keys and having Alzheimer's. If you had Alzheimer's, you wouldn't remember that you had keys. Do you understand the difference?"

I sighed, understanding the difference, but still a bit skeptical. "I guess."

"There could be any number of reasons why you are forgetting things. You're under a lot of stress at work. Do you find it hard to focus?"

"Yeah, sometimes my mind races when I think of everything I need to do."

"What about your social life?" she asked. "Are you spending time with friends?"

"Not really, I'd rather sleep on my days off."

"What about your crafts? Are you making anything interesting?"

"I have to make a special effort to work on things. It doesn't just come naturally."

"What about your moods?"

"I can't watch the evening news because it makes me cry. I always have this feeling that something bad is going to happen. And I don't understand it. I went through the worst time in my life when Renatè was sick. Now that she's recovered, I should be happy."

"Inability to focus, withdrawing from friends and family, feelings of hopelessness, being overly emotional and not having an interest in things you normally enjoy doing...Cynthia, what you've described to me are symptoms of clinical depression. I'm going to start you on a medication that will even out your moods."

The first time I took the drug, I was lying in bed and felt myself sinking down through the floor into hell. I was convinced that I heard the voice of the devil—yes, the Prince of Darkness, Satan, Beelzebub, Lucifer himself was calling my name and laughing.

The next morning, I threw the pills in the trash and called Dr. Ryan. She prescribed a different drug. Over the coming weeks, I felt like the fog was lifting. My grey days felt less foggy. After several months a sense of normalcy had been restored. I didn't cry at the slightest provocation and I was seeing my friends more instead of being such a hermit.

But several months later, when I went out of town for a conference, I forgot to pack my medicine. When I realized my mistake, I panicked at first. But then I told myself that I was only going to be gone over a weekend. I thought I'd be okay for a few days. I was wrong.

While dining with a colleague one night, I became lightheaded and nauseous. By the time dinner was over, I was doubled over in pain. Before we could get back to our hotel, I threw up on the shuttle bus. For the next two days I couldn't keep any food in my stomach, vomiting to the point of dry heaves. When I returned home, I called Dr. Ryan and told her I didn't want to be dependent on a medicine that had such control over me that I would retch without it. Dr. Ryan referred me to a psychiatrist, Dr. Mee.

COPING COCKTAIL

D r. Mee looked to be in his early thirties with brown hair and a smile that met the corners of his eyes. Despite his youth, he had already developed a reputation among his peers for being a skilled clinician. Several of my other doctors informed me that I would be in good hands in his care. Dr. Mee tried a number of drugs over the course of several years that were only minimally helpful, but he never gave up. During one of my visits, Dr. Mee asked me if I'd be interested in participating in a research study he was conducting. Wanting to be helpful, I said I'd be happy to take part. He went on to ask me a series of questions about my general health. Then he asked me a question that changed everything.

"Have you ever been a victim of sexual assault?"

I looked down at the floor and shifted in my seat. "Yes, I was raped when I was 21," I answered quietly.

Dr. Mee's eyes widened and he sat up straight in his chair. "Cynthia, I've been treating you for almost three years. Why haven't you ever mentioned this before?"

I wanted to say, "Because you never asked me before," but that would have sounded flippant, and that was not my intention.

"I never mentioned it because it has no bearing on anything," I said instead. "It happened over 25 years ago. I refuse to think about it, and I will not allow it to rule my life. If I did that, he would win."

"But you don't understand—events like this become part of our DNA. You may have set it aside in your mind, but it's still there. And it makes a difference how I will treat you now. I'd like to start you on a regimen for post-traumatic stress disorder. Are you seeing a therapist?"

"No."

"Cynthia, I strongly encourage you to do so," Dr Mee said. "The medicine will be less effective if you have feelings from the past that might be affecting your depression. Therapy can help you explore some of those feelings."

"I made my peace with the situation long ago. To dwell on it gives him power over me."

"I disagree. Therapy can actually help you take control. You'll understand yourself better when you address the source of your depression."

I had taken all the bad memories and emotions, bundled them in a neat package, and put them in a drawer in the back of my brain. Now, according to Dr. Mee, I would have to unpack those feelings if I wanted to address my depression.

I relented and agreed to meet with a therapist. Also, Dr. Mee began trying a number of medications to help me. Time has a way of collapsing in on itself when you finally achieve a goal you have been seeking. Eventually, Dr. Mee came up with the right combination of medicines that relieved my depression. I call it my *coping cocktail*. Now that I am in a good place, comfortable with my coping cocktail, looking back it doesn't seem like it took that long. In reality, it took almost three years.

Over time, Dr. Mee has helped me accept that I have a chemical imbalance that requires medication and therapy. I had to meet with several therapists before I found the right fit. For example, due to my erratic work schedule, I was late to a couple of sessions with one therapist. The therapist got really upset with me, and had no understanding for the kind of stress I was under. I didn't need the added stress of his judgment, so I stopped seeing him. Another therapist blamed all of my problems on the fact that my mother was not a nurturer. Did I wish that my mother was more supportive? Sure, but my father filled that role for me instead. The same therapist would also hug me at the end of each session. She never asked me if she could, and I didn't feel comfortable telling her that it bothered me. I had to let her go. In the end, my therapist should be someone I trust implicitly, someone who will help me explore feelings I had hidden deep inside. Searching for the best therapist made me accept that I cannot do this alone. Isolation only worsens depression.

I could pretend that the catalyst for my depression was Rentatè's near-fatal illness. Clearly, facing the prospect of her mortality had me in a tail spin. But if I am honest with myself, I have to admit the roots of my illness run much deeper.

I WILL SURVIVE

When I was a senior in college, I was raped. It resulted in a pregnancy and I had an abortion. It is not an easy thing to write about. I am by nature a private person. I didn't even tell my best friend I had been raped until many years later. The circumstances surrounding my pregnancy were complex, and I never forgave my twenty-one-year-old-self for being naïve. I now share this story in order to relinquish the shame I've felt over the years and move on with my life.

The painfully shy, socially awkward adolescent I described in an earlier chapter grew into a painfully shy, socially awkward young adult. I wasn't the "pretty one" in our family; that distinction fell to Renatè. I was the "smart one," garnering mostly A's and accolades throughout my school life. I spent a lot of time in the library, and other than a small circle of friends, I kept to myself. Boys never asked me out, so I didn't date in high school.

I met the man that later became my first boyfriend at an after-hours coffee shop one Saturday night. He was 5'9" with a dark complexion and eyes that sparkled when he smiled. Having been a Golden Gloves boxing champion, his build was muscular. He had a quick wit and could make me smile regardless of what my mood was. He called me by my last name and when he said it, it sounded so sweet that my heart would melt like butter in the sun.

Within a few weeks, we were spending all of our spare time together. He was a military police officer (MP) assigned to the jail at Fort Riley. I refer to him as MP because in the end, his job was the one quality about him that I still admire. I had been a student at Kansas State University working toward a pre-law/political science degree. Our schedules only allowed for us to be together evenings and some weekends depending on his duty assignments, and as a result, he would often sleep overnight at my apartment. My parents had instilled in me the concept that pre-marital sex was a sin. I told MP I didn't want to go to hell, so at night we only cuddled.

I was drawn to MP because of his sweet personality and because he treated me like a queen, often bringing me flowers, jewelry and other gifts. He was physically affectionate and constantly told me how beautiful and sexy I was. No one had ever said those things to me before. Twenty-one-year-old me was flattered.

But several months into the relationship, I felt like I was suffocating. He was so intense. When we were together, he always had his arms around me, smothering me with kisses. He talked a lot about our future and how he wanted a family, and while I knew I wanted children someday, I wasn't thinking that far into the future. I was focused on finishing my last semester, getting my Bachelor's degree, and starting law school.

One morning, I awoke and felt a searing pain in my pelvis. At first I thought it was menstrual cramps, but because I wasn't due for another week, I dismissed the idea. I was still groggy from sleep, but as I became more awake, I realized that MP was on top of me. I was lying on my stomach and the weight of his body made it hard for me to breathe. I was shocked when I realized his penis was inside me.

"What are you doing?" I cried. "Get off me!" With all my strength, I tried to push up, but my arms were like spaghetti. His muscular build was too much for me. He didn't budge. Finally, after a few minutes of struggling, he let out a guttural moan, removed his limp penis and rolled off of me. I got out of bed.

"You were lying there," he said. "Your body is just so sexy, I couldn't help myself."

"Have you lost your mind?" I yelled. "Get out!"

He continued to try to talk, but I was so outraged I ignored his words. Finally he collected his belongings and left.

I stood there shaking, not wanting to believe what had just happened. I immediately ran into the shower, needing to rid myself of his smell. I stood under the hot water and scrubbed my skin, but unfortunately I couldn't wash away the pain in my vagina—the remaining evidence. Otherwise, I could pretend like the assault didn't happen. And that's how I thought of it: as an assault. It would be many years before I could admit to myself that it was rape. Rape was too intimate and personal. Even more painful was the realization that I had been betrayed by a man that I trusted.

After I showered, I dressed and got ready to go to class. The Kansas wind had been brutal that day. Or maybe it was just that I felt so vulnerable. It was as if my body was a sieve. I sat through my classes, but had little retention of what the instructors said. I was determined not to allow the rape to affect me. I felt that if it did, it meant he won.

I didn't speak to MP for weeks. He called several times a day. I allowed the answering machine to pick up. He left messages begging me to forgive him. Sometimes he'd say that he just wanted to talk with me so he could explain himself, but other times he left angry messages calling me a bitch for not talking to him. When I didn't return his calls, he started coming by my apartment, and on one occasion he stood outside my door calling my name.

"Doss, I know you're in there!" I heard him call. "Please just talk to me. I know I messed up, but you have to talk to me."

It was winter with two feet of snow on the ground, but that didn't deter him from staying almost an hour trying to get me to come to the door. I lay on my couch with a pillow over my ears trying to drown out the sound of his voice. He repeated this episode several times a week. His behavior scared me. I didn't know what he would do next. I only left my apartment when absolutely necessary for fear I would run into him. I was also angry. He had made me a prisoner in my own home.

One morning, I got up and felt sick to my stomach and dizzy. I broke out in a cold sweat. It was January—flu season—so I went to the student health office. They ran some tests and instead of prescribing an antibiotic, the doctor told me I was pregnant.

I felt as though a dagger had pierced my heart. My limbs were numb as if all the blood had drained from them. The doctor, an attractive man in his early 30's, had a very compassionate bedside manner.

"I know this is a lot for you to absorb, but I want you to know that you have options," he said. "If you decide to have the baby, I'll prescribe some prenatal vitamins for you and I have some brochures on adoption that I can give you. If not, I can refer you to a clinic in Kansas City. You don't have to decide now. Take some time and think about it."

I knew what he was referring to when he mentioned the clinic. It was 1979; six years after the landmark U.S. Supreme Court decision in the case Roe v Wade legalized abortion.

I didn't tell the doctor, but I was pretty certain I knew what I had to do. If I had a baby, I would have to postpone finishing my degree and it would be impossible to go to law school. I came from a small town that didn't offer many good job opportunities, and the most I could expect would be a minimum wage position. I considered what it would be like to raise a child as a single parent with no money. Adoption was out of the question; I couldn't see having a child of mine raised by someone else. No, I could not have a baby. More importantly, I could not have MP's baby. His behavior had proven him to be emotionally and mentally unstable, and having his child would link me to him for the rest of my life.

The next time MP called, I answered the phone.

"I'm pregnant," was all I said.

"I know."

"What do you mean you know?"

"Well, I had my suspicions. Doss, I tracked your periods and I guessed when you'd be ovulating. You said you wanted to have a family while you were young. This is a blessing. The two of us are going to be parents."

If I had any doubts about my decision, they disintegrated completely after hearing MP's admission. I realized how delusional he was, and that he lived in a twisted universe if he thought his behavior was acceptable. I knew I needed to get as far away from him as possible.

"How dare you make a decision like that for me?" I demanded. "You had no right."

"I want us to have a future together. Doss, you'll be finishing school soon, and I've never been to college. You'll be starting your career, so where does that leave me? All those things I told you about my family weren't true. My father doesn't own a liquor store. He's just a clerk there. I said that to impress you. I was afraid of losing you."

"Your plan was wrong on so many levels and in the end, it didn't work. I'm not having the baby. There's a clinic where I can have an abortion."

"Doss, you can't."

"I can and I will. Goodbye, MP."

That was our last conversation. He still called several times a day and came by my apartment for weeks. I was lucky that my landlord didn't live onsite because MP created such a disturbance at my door, and I was afraid I was going to get evicted. I never responded to his calls or answered the door. I had nothing left to say to him and I was through listening. He was a liar, a manipulator and a rapist.

THE RIGHT TO CHOOSE

My emotions ran the gamut from defiance to debilitating fear. At times, I was confident that I wasn't going to let my predicament ruin my life, but there were also times when I would be curled up on my couch unable to do anything or go anywhere. When I did make it to campus, I would pass groups of people and imagine that they were talking about me. The slightest noise would make me jump, and I seemed to always be cold. On the way to my biology class, I had to pass a display in the hallway. About a dozen gallon jars lined the walls, each holding preserved fetuses in different stages of development. I had always found the display disturbing. It lacked dignity, like something in a carnival freak show. Now that I was pregnant, I was incensed by it.

If I were going to have a child, it would need to be on my terms. I would need to be established in my career and married in a committed, stable relationship with the father, a compassionate man that shared my commitment to providing a loving, secure environment for our children. Now that I look back on the situation, I am even more confident that I made the right decision. MP was not the man I envisioned as the father of my children.

That man would be like my father—a man who put others' needs ahead of his own. My father was even-tempered and never held a grudge. If he got mad at me for something I did, it didn't last long. He had an infinite capacity to forgive people and let go of the past. He was a caring man, fiercely protective of his family. If any of us had a problem, we knew we could count on him to listen and provide sound guidance.

Therefore, it was natural that I would want to talk to my father first about my predicament. Sitting on the couch in my dark basement apartment, I dialed the first few numbers on my rotary phone, and then hung up. I did this several times. My shoulders were hunched over, my stomach churned, and I had a bitter taste in my mouth. Finally, I took a deep breath and completed the number.

"Hi, Daddy, it's me."

"Hey, Buddy," he said. "How are you?"

"Not so good."

"Are you having trouble with your classes?"

"No, well, yes. Biology is kicking my butt. I've got a midterm exam next week. But that's not what I mean."

"What's wrong?"

There was silence as I gathered my thoughts and tried to form the right words in my head. How could I tell him I had failed to safeguard my virtue, one of the most important rules my parents taught me? It didn't matter that I had been raped; I felt I never should have trusted MP. I should have known he was devious. After all, my sister was the "pretty daughter", and I was the "smart daughter". It was the core of who I was, and I felt I was nothing without my intellect. I would rather my parents think I had been careless than to admit I had been outwitted by a man. It wasn't until years later that I realized

I was not at fault. MP had given me no reason not to trust him. He was, by all appearances, a sweet passionate man. I had done nothing wrong.

Still, that night, sitting in my basement apartment while my father waited for my response, the words swelled in my throat and I began to cry.

"Ah, come on now buddy," he said. "Don't cry. Tell me what's wrong." His voice was calm and soothing as always.

When I finished sobbing, I said, "Daddy, I'm pregnant." I wrapped the phone cord around my index finger in the silence that followed.

"Who's the father, MP?"

"Yes , sir. And Daddy ever since I broke up with him, he's been coming by my apartment banging on the door trying to get me to come out. Sometimes he leaves messages on my answering machine calling me all kinds of nasty names. Then other times, he says how much he loves me and wants me back. Daddy, I don't think he's stable and I certainly don't think he's suitable to be a good father. How can I raise a child with a father that's unstable?" *And not to mention a rapist.*

"Well, ultimately it's your decision. I trust your judgment and I'm here to help you whatever you decide," Daddy said. "But we have to tell your mother now."

"I know, but I'm a mess. Let me call you guys tomorrow."

My father always knew the right words to say. After talking to him, my shoulders felt lighter. I sat up straighter with my chest open. But I couldn't relax yet. I needed to prepare for breaking the news to my mother. I knew her first response would be how this news would reflect on *her*. I couldn't cry like I did with my father.

The following day with both my parents on the phone, I told my mother the news. I had rehearsed every word so that my voice would be even. I even paced up and down my living room floor so that my body wouldn't shake from nervousness. Facing the prospect of having an abortion was scary, but having to tell my mother I was pregnant was the hardest thing I had ever done in my young life.

Her first question was, "Who all knows about this?"

"Only MP and my friend Valerie know," I said. "No one else."

"Let's keep it that way. What are you going to do?"

"Student Health gave me a referral to an abortion clinic in Kansas City. I'll call Curtis and see if he can take me." Curtis was in law school at the time at the University of Kansas in Lawrence, about 45 minutes from Kansas City.

"That's a good idea," she replied. "Call Curtis and make the arrangements with the clinic."

It didn't surprise me that my mother didn't ask how I was doing, but that didn't mean it hurt any less. I felt a throbbing pain in my chest. She must have known that I was scared, that I could have used some reassuring words. But she was more pragmatic than that. There was a problem and I had a solution—*that's* what mattered most to her.

What was more important was what she didn't say. She didn't tell me I had been irresponsible, although I imagined that was what she told my father after they got off the phone. And in the years to come, she wouldn't use the term pregnancy, but she never missed an opportunity to remind me of my "mistake".

As it turned out, having Curtis take me to the clinic was a great idea. He was the perfect person for me to be with at that time. He listened attentively when I talked and respected my silence when I withdrew. I was close enough to Curtis to share my deepest feelings, while my other brother Cyril offered a different kind of support. When I told him about MP's menacing phone calls and visits and he said, "I can send a couple of guys to rough up MP if you want. They'll be in and out of the state before anyone even knows they were there."

We joked about his offer, and though it was tempting, I didn't want him to risk assault charges on my account. I don't recall ever discussing the pregnancy with Renatè. At the time, we weren't very close. If she had an opinion about my predicament, she never shared it.

A TOUGH DECISION

On the morning of the procedure, I was famished. I wasn't allowed to eat anything for eight hours in advance.

"I feel like I could eat a cow," I told Curtis in the car on the way to the clinic.

"Our first stop will be White Castle when you are done," he suggested.

"Sounds like a plan."

I only have a few memories of the clinic—mostly I've tried to block it out of my mind—but I do recall that the staff was professional and caring. I remember feeling the pinch of the needle from the local anesthetic. I remember the humming sound of the vacuum when the doctor began, a sound that ordinarily would have a calming effect, but in this case it quickened my heartbeat. With each undulating movement of my pelvis, I reminded myself this was the only choice that made sense. I had to rid myself of any connection to MP and his manic episodes outside my apartment. I had to protect my future.

When I was finished, Curtis and I walked silently to the car.

"Next stop, White Castle," he declared as he got behind the wheel of the car.

"I'm not hungry. Can we just go home?"

"Sure, anything you want."

At his apartment, I immediately took off my clothes and climbed into bed. Curtis brought me a bowl of soup, saying that I needed to eat something. He sat with me quietly as I finished the soup.

"I'll let you get some rest," he said as he removed the tray and left the room.

I curled my legs up and pulled the covers over my head. Then I cried. Other than the conversation with my father, it was the only time I ever allowed myself to cry for the not-yet-living.

After the abortion, I got an infection that left me weak. In addition, the doctor had prescribed a sedative for me, and when taking it, I was unable to go on campus some days. I took an incomplete grade in two of my classes, which meant I wasn't able to graduate with my classmates. But I never lost sight of my goal. I was able to finish the classes in summer session and got my degree. Being focused on my goals was what helped me through those difficult times.

I never talked about my abortion out of fear that people would disagree with my decision. Some people that know me may be shocked, but recently it occurred to me I don't really give a shit if other people try to stand in judgment of me. People that know me well understand that I would not have made such a decision without carefully weighing the consequences. Fortunately, my network of friends is nurturing and supportive, and I have no room in my life for detractors. Besides, I alone will stand before God on judgment day. I am confident I made the right decision.

For several years after I graduated college, I worked for social service organizations. I learned about a rape crisis intervention team and decided to volunteer. In our training, we were exposed to what a victim experiences dealing with medical and mental health professionals, law enforcement and the courts to help prepare us to provide support for the victim. After several years of volunteering for a rape crisis intervention team, I could finally admit that I had been raped. By helping others, I was able to heal myself. My only regret is that my parents will never know that I had been raped. My mother and father have passed on. That saddens me. It also saddens me that I never had the opportunity to have a child on my terms since I never married. And at age sixty, I'm not likely to become a parent, and there will always be a void space in my heart that nothing else can fill. It is painful, but I have accepted that having children simply was not my fate.

For years, I felt ashamed that I had been such a poor judge of character in allowing MP into my life and into my bed. MP wanted to control my life and determine my destiny; in a way, he did. He may have changed the circumstances of my life, but he didn't change the course of it. I determined that. Telling this story allows me to relinquish the shame of being naïve. It no longer has any power over me, and I can forgive my twenty-one-year-old self and commend her for having courage in arduous circumstances.

Over the years, I struggled to maintain a positive outlook despite having such a devastating event occur early in life. Through therapy, I could look back on the tragic times in my life with wise eyes and put them in perspective. I learned that I am stronger and more capable than I thought I was at the time. The coping skills I learned when I had the abortion helped me deal with Renatè's illness, too. I stayed focused on the idea that she would recover and we would vacation in Germany, the country of her birth next.

My *coping cocktail* has also helped, but the drugs aren't a panacea. I still have my low periods, and it didn't help that my work was always stressful. For fifteen years, I maintained an erratic work schedule, and it played havoc with my sleep. I suffered from chronic insomnia that still plagues me today.

I had reached a point where I was doing so much for others in my work and personal life and not doing anything for myself. Then a unique opportunity presented itself, one where I could do something special for Cynthia. I felt I couldn't pass it up.

ONE STEP

I stood in the open doorway of the plane. Before me, I saw blue sky for miles. Below me were wispy clouds and 12,000 feet of open sky. My instructor, Greg gave me my final instruction.

"Take one step forward and leave the rest to me," he said.

In a whirlwind of thoughts, my reason for being there suddenly occurred to me:

This is what you've been yearning for. It's time for the ultimate test.

I thought about the circumstances that brought me to that point—and how the best ideas always begin with margaritas.

"It was the most incredible thing I've ever done," one of my colleagues said, glowing with excitement as she took another sip of her margarita. A group of us were at an Irish pub after an all-day seminar and winding down with a few drinks. We were talking about unusual experiences, and she mentioned hers from a few years previously: skydiving.

"Wow, it must take years of experience to learn to skydive," I said. "That's real dedication."

"No, it was a tandem jump," she said. "You have an instructor strapped to your back, and he does everything—you're just along for the ride." She brushed her long brown hair away from her face, her amber eyes bright with energy. I had only met this colleague earlier that day, and from our interactions in the seminar, I took her to be on the conservative side. I was surprised to see this more carefree side of her, and became even more fascinated by her story.

"Weren't you afraid?" I asked.

"Sure, I'd be crazy not to be a little scared," she replied, "but I went through an orientation first. They told me exactly what to expect and the instructor gave me all the safety precautions. The whole time, the instructors are joking and laughing. They made it a fun experience while at the same time calming our fears. The instructors are really well-built, too. I have to admit, having a buff guy strapped to my back was a plus."

"Cool," I laughed. "Then what happened?"

"I boarded the plane. We took off and when we reached the right altitude, the instructor walked me to the edge of the door, and we stepped out."

"You make it sound so simple."

"It was. And floating in the sky was the most amazing feeling I have ever experienced."

For months, I thought about my colleague's experience. I became obsessed with the idea of skydiving, which was uncharacteristic for me. I've always played it safe, not to mention I was petrified of heights. Still, I felt compelled to skydive. As luck would have it, the alumni chapter of our sorority was scheduled to go to a conference in Las Vegas, close to the airfield where my colleague had jumped.

I made a reservation at the airfield, but I didn't share my plans with my sorority sisters. I thought they would say it was too dangerous. Instead, I left a note in my hotel room in case someone needed to claim my body. It said:

Renatè,

My will is in the shoe box in the spare bedroom closet.

Give my love to Mommy and Daddy. Love, Cyn

I put on my best outfit, a Donna Karan red and white floral-print jean jacket with coordinating red jeans. If something was going to happen, I was going out in style.

When I got to the airfield, they gave us an orientation and paired us up with our instructors. The instructor helping me put on the gear was old as Methuselah. I thought, *This can't be right. He looks like he would have a heart attack if he stepped out of a plane.*

I grew increasingly nervous as he helped me into my jumpsuit. *I'm supposed to put my life in the hands of this guy? This is not what I signed up for.*

Then two muscle bound men burst through the front door. They checked in at the front desk and one of them approached me. He thanked Methuselah for covering for him.

"Hi, my name is Greg," he told me while giving my hand a shake. "I'll be your instructor today." He was 6'2" tall with long sandy blonde hair. His t-shirt showed off his well-defined pectoral muscles and washboard abs. His biceps were the size of bowling balls.

Now this is more like it!

Greg finished suiting me up and we walked out to the plane. Before we boarded, each student had to pose for a picture giving the thumbs-up sign. They weren't just selling the jump; they also offered photos, a videotape and souvenirs for purchase. I signed up for the full package which also included a commemorative t-shirt that said, *"Why gamble your money when you can gamble your life?"*

The plane's fuselage was empty except for two long benches. We filed in and took our seats. I heard a series of snaps as Greg fastened his harness to my back. Now, the situation became real. I was going to jump out of a plane and fall 12,000 feet. I got a lump in my throat.

The plane took off down the runway. I closed my eyes like I always do during a take-off, so that I can tell the exact moment the wheels leave the pavement and we become airborne. I once read that scientists have studied the design of bumble bees and can offer no explanation for why they can fly, because the bumble bee's size, weight and the shape of its body are all wrong in relation to its total wingspread. I wondered if the same were true of planes. Was there a mystic force behind the miracle of airplane flight?

An instructor to my right must have thought I was praying, because when I opened my eyes, he put his hand on my arm and looked at me earnestly. "You're going to be just fine," he said. "Don't worry." Then he said something silly that made me laugh. The rest of the instructors were making the students laugh by joking that this was their first jump, too. It was a welcome distraction from the noise of the engine and the vibration that jostled me around. I detected the faint smell of fuel in the air—or maybe it was fear.

When we reached the appropriate altitude, the first pair in front of me stood up and moved to the open door, vanishing in a flash. We moved forward down the bench. I looked down at my hands; they were visibly shaking. I clasped them together to stop the movement as the second pair moved to the door and vanished, as well. We inched forward on the bench.

Before I knew it, it was our turn, with Greg reassuring me as we made our way to the door. I couldn't believe my feet were taking me toward the mother of all steps—toward answers.

I looked down at the parceled landscape below, sprawled before me and resembling a Monopoly game board. Most of what I saw was desert and a small mountain range, but the view was spectacular. Peering out of six inch square airplane window had paled in comparison; now I could see for miles.

This is what you've been yearning for.

I shook my head to cast off the doubt and stepped out into the open sky. In a second, we were airborne. It felt like we were lying weightlessly on a bed of cotton. If not for the clouds moving past us, I would have thought we were floating instead of falling. Later, I would learn that in free-fall, we were probably traveling 120 miles per hour!

The roar of the plane's engine faded away. Then...

Silence

It was a type of silence I had never experienced before. The absence of any discernible noise made the rest of my senses more acute. I could feel my heart pounding a staccato rhythm in my chest. The air was soft and cool against my face, gently caressing my whole body and completely relaxing my muscles. It was like getting a full body massage with my clothes on. Nothing could compare to that feeling of being unfettered.

Greg's voice broke the silence. "How you doing, Cynthia?" He had to bend close to my ear for me to hear him.

"I'm great! This is amazing!"

"Just relax and enjoy the ride."

I relished every second of it. We were in free-fall for only a minute, but those sixty seconds were glorious. When it came time for Greg to open the parachute he tilted his head toward mine once again.

"There'll be a huge jerk and then we'll fly up. But don't worry, we'll be perfectly safe."

I was so captivated by the view that it took me a while to realize that Greg was shouting my name. I thought it was strange because he had only spoken to me calmly before. I didn't realize what had happened until later when I saw the video. In my excitement, I was gripping the harness so tightly he couldn't pull the ripcord. Finally he was able to get my attention and deployed the parachute.

We were in a seated position after the parachute deployed, and I could remember sitting on swings as a kid. Back then, I was always afraid to go too high, but now I was thousands of feet in the air and I wasn't nervous. I felt free. I didn't think about Renatè's almost fatal illness, my aging parents or the stress at work. I wasn't worried about the problems of the past or the challenges I might face in the future. Only the present mattered.

"Would you like to steer the parachute?" I heard Greg ask.

I nodded, and he handed me the reins that allowed me to change direction. We were surrounded by miles of open sky, and for once, I had control over my own destiny. I felt perfectly safe, my whole body tingling with excitement. Taking it all in, I savored every moment.

As the ground grew closer and closer, Greg told me to keep my legs forward. "We're going to land sitting down," he said, and he was right; we ended up landing with the ease of sitting down at a picnic.

Methuselah was there to greet us, and he helped Greg disconnect the parachute and take off my gear. I immediately gave Greg a great big bear hug and thanked him.

"Don't you want to do it again?" asked Methuselah.

I frowned and looked at him thinking, *Why would I want to do it again? I accomplished my goal.* Instead I smiled and told him, "No, thank you. It was the experience of a lifetime."

My feet were planted firmly on the ground, but my heart was still in the sky. I had stepped out of an airplane at 12,000 feet and fell to the earth at an alarming speed. The sense of freedom I felt in that moment remains unparalleled by any other experience I have ever had.

At the time, I didn't question why I felt compelled to jump. Upon reflection years later, I can see the reasons clearly. So much of what was happening at that point in my life had been beyond my control. Renatè had the near-fatal Sickle Cell crisis and continuing medical problems; my mother had a seizure; and my father's was exhibiting more symptoms of Alzheimer's disease. But with that jump, I took control. I alone decided to make the jump—no one talked me into it and I wouldn't allow anyone to talk me out of it.

Also, I needed to know that I could get through the traumatic events in my life and that everything would be all right. I faced my fear of heights straight on, taking a dramatic leap of faith and surviving. When facing a scary situation in the future, I could look back on that experience and channel the euphoria I felt on the jump to get me through it. I now knew that it was within my power to thrive.

EPILOGUE

In time, I have reconciled my feelings about Renatè's illness. The prospect of losing my sister - my best friend - devastated me. I couldn't talk to the people I would normally discuss my feelings with—my parents—because they were facing their own fears with their daughter comatose in the hospital. In fact, we seldom talked about the episode, and when we did, we referred to it as "Renatè's nap." But I did have friends that I could talk to, and being able to acknowledge how much fear and loneliness I experienced at the time helped me.

For a long time I was angry with Mommy for not helping us watch over Renatè. Maintaining that vigil by her bedside had been physically and emotionally draining. Then I realized that as a mother, it must have been painful to watch her child without being able to do anything to help her but pray. Besides, the lessons that Cyril and I had learned from our mother growing up helped us be advocates in her absence. And she was far from useless during those days. Mommy's role had been to entertain guests in the waiting room, keeping up the polite conversations for which I didn't have the stomach or patience.

But I was also angry with Mommy for blaming me for Renatè's illness. I've since learned that in a crisis, people struggle to make sense of the unknown. Assigning blame gives a person a false sense of power over a situation that in reality is beyond their control. Mommy thought there had to be an explanation for Renatè's illness and our trip to the Bahamas seemed a likely culprit. In her desire to rationalize the situation, she failed to realize what a burden she placed on me. Ultimately, I had to let go of my anger in order to have peace within myself and forgive her.

My world changed dramatically when I learned that the source of my feelings of loss was clinical depression. Because I had humility drilled into me growing up, I found it hard to focus on myself. It was one of the reasons Renatè's illness hit me so hard—because I was so accustomed to focusing on her and protecting her. I didn't recognize the symptoms because I cared more about looking after her well-being than I did my own, and I was depressed for years before being diagnosed.

Though the combination of therapy and my *coping cocktail* have made life bearable, I still have challenges. It was difficult to watch as Daddy's Alzheimer's disease progressed to the level where he no longer had the ability to communicate in coherent sentences. When I saw him like that, I felt an anvil pressing against my chest. He was a man that was intelligent, creative, and a whiz at fixing things, but during a visit before he passed away, I watched him try to eat his soup with a fork. In a very selfish way, I also grieve for the loss of a man that was my biggest fan. Luckily, his personality did not change, and for that I am grateful. Up until his death, he still smiled while he talked, and laughed at his own jokes. Even though I didn't understand him, I laughed with him.

It has been twenty-one years since Renatè's phenomenal recovery. Time and emotional distance have given me objectivity, and my "Aha!" moment came when I realized that I was not responsible. I did not cause Renatè's illness. The doctors never determined why SCA attacked so many of her systems and our trip to the Bahamas may or may not have exposed her to danger. There was nothing I could have done more to protect her. Also, I finally accepted it was not within my power to cure her. All I could do was pray and leave her recovery in God's hands.

However, the greatest lesson I learned was that it is okay to be afraid. Life can present us with frightening circumstances. I find comfort in a poem from Mary Anne Radmacher-Hershey that Renatè has hanging in her office. The poem ends with, "Courage doesn't always roar. Sometimes it is the quiet voice at the end of the day saying 'I'll try again tomorrow.'"